ALTO SAX 365

BY AARON GARDNER

I0828478

HOW TO GET THE AUDIO	3
INTRODUCTION	4
TRILL CHART	5
FINGERING CHART	6
WEEK 1: C MAJOR	**8**
WEEK 2: F MAJOR	**10**
WEEK 3: G MAJOR	**12**
WEEK 4: B♭ MAJOR	**14**
WEEK 5: D MAJOR	**16**
WEEK 6: E♭ MAJOR	**18**
WEEK 7: A MAJOR	**20**
WEEK 8: A♭ MAJOR	**22**
WEEK 9: E MAJOR	**24**
WEEK 10: D♭ MAJOR	**26**
WEEK 11: B MAJOR	**28**
WEEK 12: F♯ MAJOR	**30**
WEEK 13: REVIEW 1	**32**
WEEK 14: C NATURAL MINOR	**34**
WEEK 15: G NATURAL MINOR	**37**
WEEK 16: B♭ NATURAL MINOR	**39**
WEEK 17: F NATURAL MINOR	**41**
WEEK 18: D NATURAL MINOR	**43**
WEEK 19: E♭ NATURAL MINOR	**45**
WEEK 20: A NATURAL MINOR	**47**
WEEK 21: A♭ NATURAL MINOR	**49**
WEEK 22: E NATURAL MINOR	**51**

ISBN: 978-1-969094-21-7

WEEK 23: C♯ NATURAL MINOR	**53**
WEEK 24: B NATURAL MINOR	**56**
WEEK 25: F♯ NATURAL MINOR	**59**
WEEK 26: REVIEW 2	**61**
WEEK 27: C HARMONIC MINOR	**64**
WEEK 28: F HARMONIC MINOR	**67**
WEEK 29: G HARMONIC MINOR	**69**
WEEK 30: B♭ HARMONIC MINOR	**72**
WEEK 31: D HARMONIC MINOR	**75**
WEEK 32: E♭ HARMONIC MINOR	**78**
WEEK 33: A HARMONIC MINOR	**81**
WEEK 34: A♭ HARMONIC MINOR	**83**
WEEK 35: E HARMONIC MINOR	**86**
WEEK 36: C♯ HARMONIC MINOR	**89**
WEEK 37: B HARMONIC MINOR	**92**
WEEK 38: F♯ HARMONIC MINOR	**94**
WEEK 39: REVIEW 3	**97**
WEEK 40: C BLUES SCALE	**100**
WEEK 41: F & G BLUES SCALES	**102**
WEEK 42: B♭ & D BLUES SCALES	**105**
WEEK 43: E♭ & A BLUES SCALES	**108**
WEEK 44: E & C♯ BLUES SCALES	**111**
WEEK 45: B & F♯ BLUES SCALES	**113**
WEEK 46: C & B♭ MAJOR ii–V–I	**116**
WEEK 47: F & E♭ MAJOR ii–V–I	**119**
WEEK 48: A & G MAJOR ii–V–I	**122**
WEEK 49: E & D MAJOR ii–V–I	**125**
WEEK 50: C♯ & B MAJOR ii–V–I	**128**
WEEK 51: A♭ & F♯ MAJOR ii–V–I	**131**
WEEK 52: REVIEW 4	**134**
WEEK 53: DAY 365	**137**
ABOUT THE AUTHOR	138

HOW TO GET THE AUDIO

The audio files for this book are available for free as downloads or streaming on *troynelsonmusic.com*.

We are available to help you with your audio downloads and any other questions you may have. Simply email *help@troynelsonmusic.com*.

See below for the recommended ways to listen to the audio:

Download Audio Files

- Download Audio Files (Zipped)
- Recommended for COMPUTERS on WiFi
- A ZIP file will automatically download to the default "downloads" folder on your computer
- Recommended: download to a desktop/laptop computer *first*, then transfer to a tablet or cell phone
- Phones & tablets may need an "unzipping" app such as iZip, Unrar or Winzip
- Download on WiFi for faster download speeds

Stream Audio Files

- Recommended for CELL PHONES & TABLETS
- Bookmark this page
- Simply tap the PLAY button on the track you want to listen to
- Files also available for streaming or download at *soundcloud.com/troynelsonbooks*

To download the companion audio files for this book, visit: troynelsonmusic.com/audio-downloads/

INTRODUCTION

Welcome to *Alto Sax 365*. You have just punched your ticket for a one-year adventure that will lead to better saxophone playing. In this book, you will find everything you need to improve your playing. The daily exercises include scales, long tones, technique, intervals, articulation, theory, dynamics, and ornamentation, as well as musical pieces to work on and play.

This book is intended to supplement and inspire your regular daily practice, as there are exercises for every day of an entire year. The days are divided by category; for example, Mondays are long-tone exercise days. On each Sunday, you will have a musical piece to work on that incorporates elements from the exercises of that week. All of these pieces are relatively short and most can be completed in about 15-to-30 minutes.

The book increases in difficulty as you move through it: It starts at a beginner-to-intermediate level, and by the end, you'll be working at a more advanced level. When working with a book of this nature, it's important that you have a firm grasp on each piece before moving onto the next. Some of the later exercises may take a little more work and time to perfect.

Included are audio tracks that I have personally recorded for each exercise and musical piece in the book. You should listen to these before working on the exercises. Once you have sufficiently practiced the exercise, try playing along with the recordings.

This book is designed to be a practical and useful tool for musicians of all levels and styles. Most of the early exercises are based on classical music, but towards the end of the book, you will find exercises in blues and jazz styles. This book can also be a great motivator to achieve daily practice on your instrument, which is the best way to build good technique and sound on your horn.

Here are some tips on how to work through this book:

- Make sure your instrument is in good working condition. Equipment problems can make playing very frustrating. Also, find a comfortable, quiet place to practice, one that is free from interruptions and devices.

- Start each exercise slowly, gradually increasing the tempo as you work on it.

- Don't be too critical of how you sound at first. You can always go back and work on those exercises again.

- Don't be afraid to experiment. Play each exercise in different ways and with different feels. Above all… HAVE FUN!

I sincerely hope that you enjoy this book and find it a useful supplement to your studies. It has been educational and enjoyable to write, and I'm excited to share it with you.

TRILL CHART

F–F♯
A♭–B♭
B♭–B
B♭–C
B–C
tr
tr
tr
tr
tr
White = open
Black = pressed
Gray = move rapidly to produce the trill
C–D
C♯–D
C♯–E
D♭–E♭
D♯–E
E♭–F
tr
tr
tr
tr
tr
tr
E♭–F♯
F–F♯
F♯–G♯
B♭–C
D♭–E♭
tr
tr
tr
tr
tr

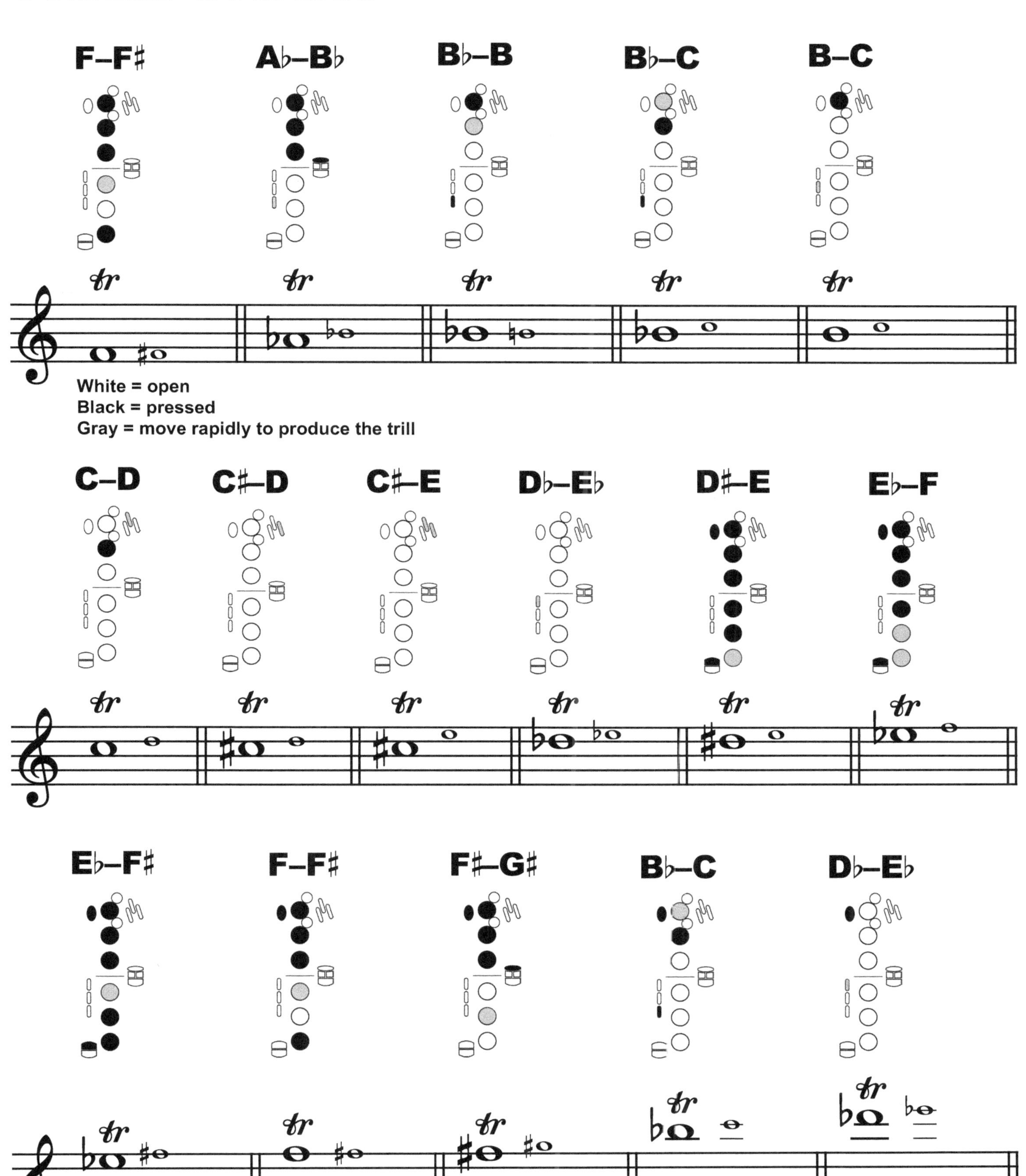

FINGERING CHART

A♯/B♭
B
C
C♯/D♭
D

White = open
Black = pressed

D♯/E♭
E
F
F♯/G♭
G

G♯/A♭
A
A♯/B♭
B
C

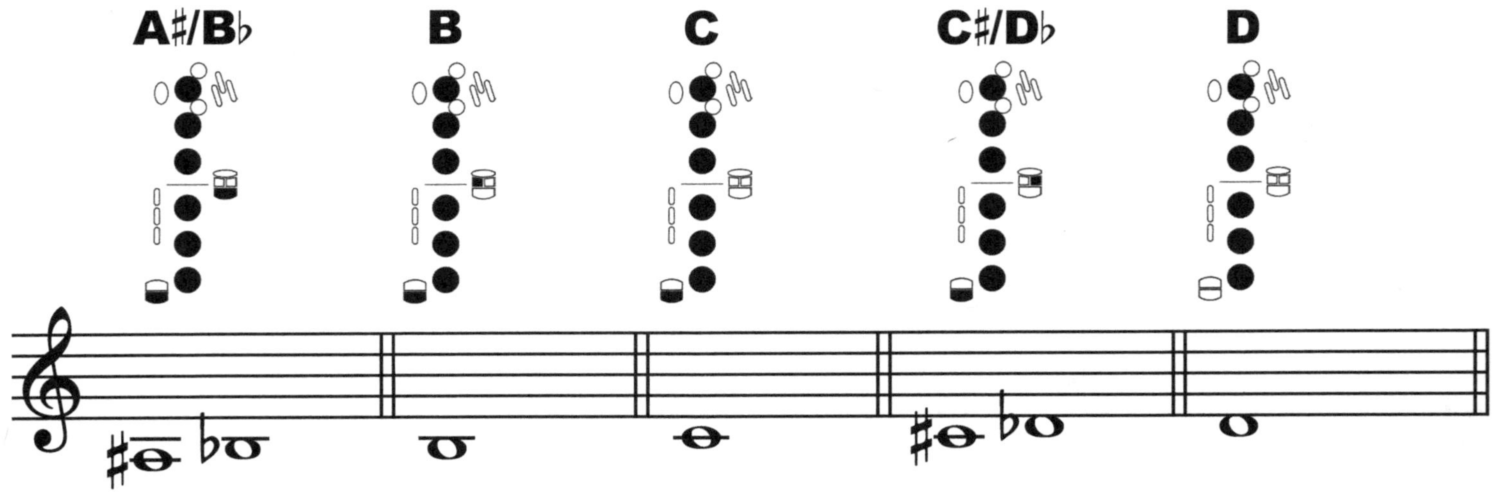

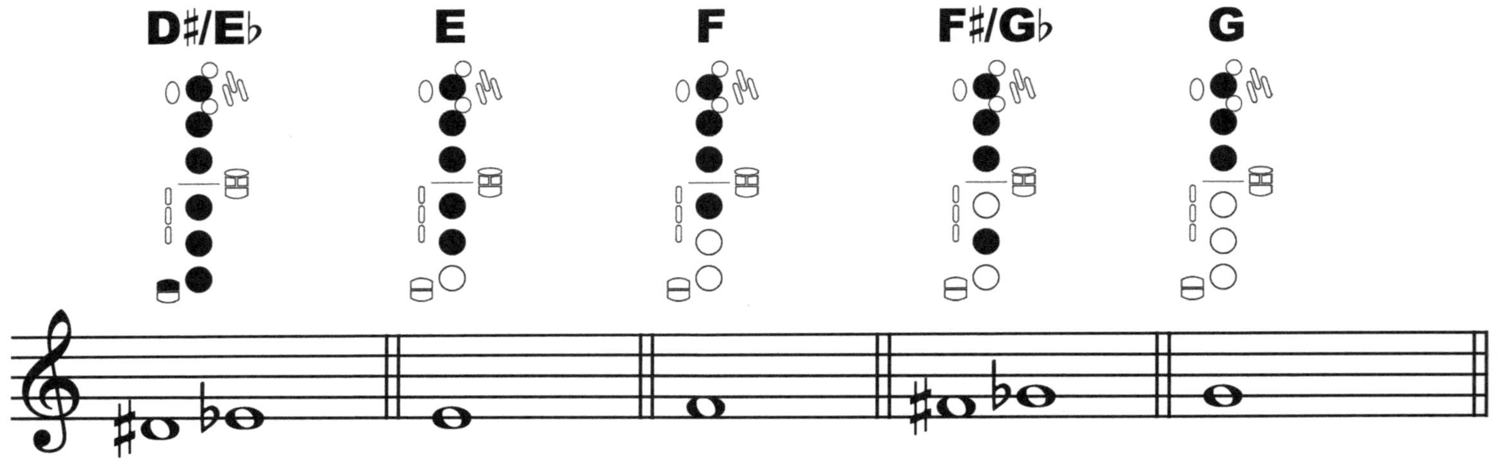

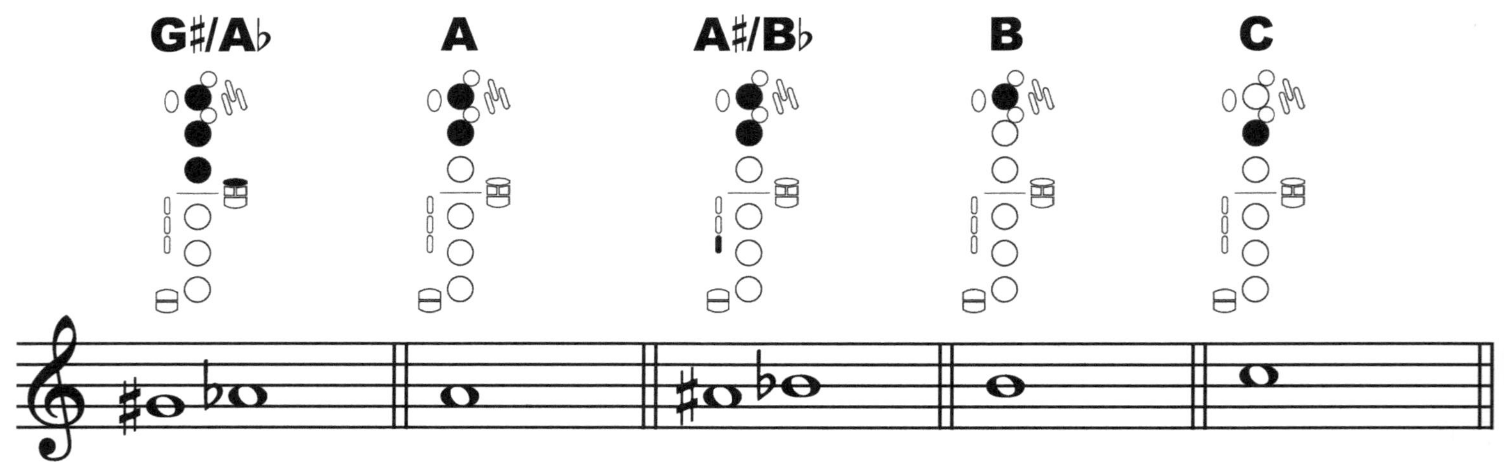

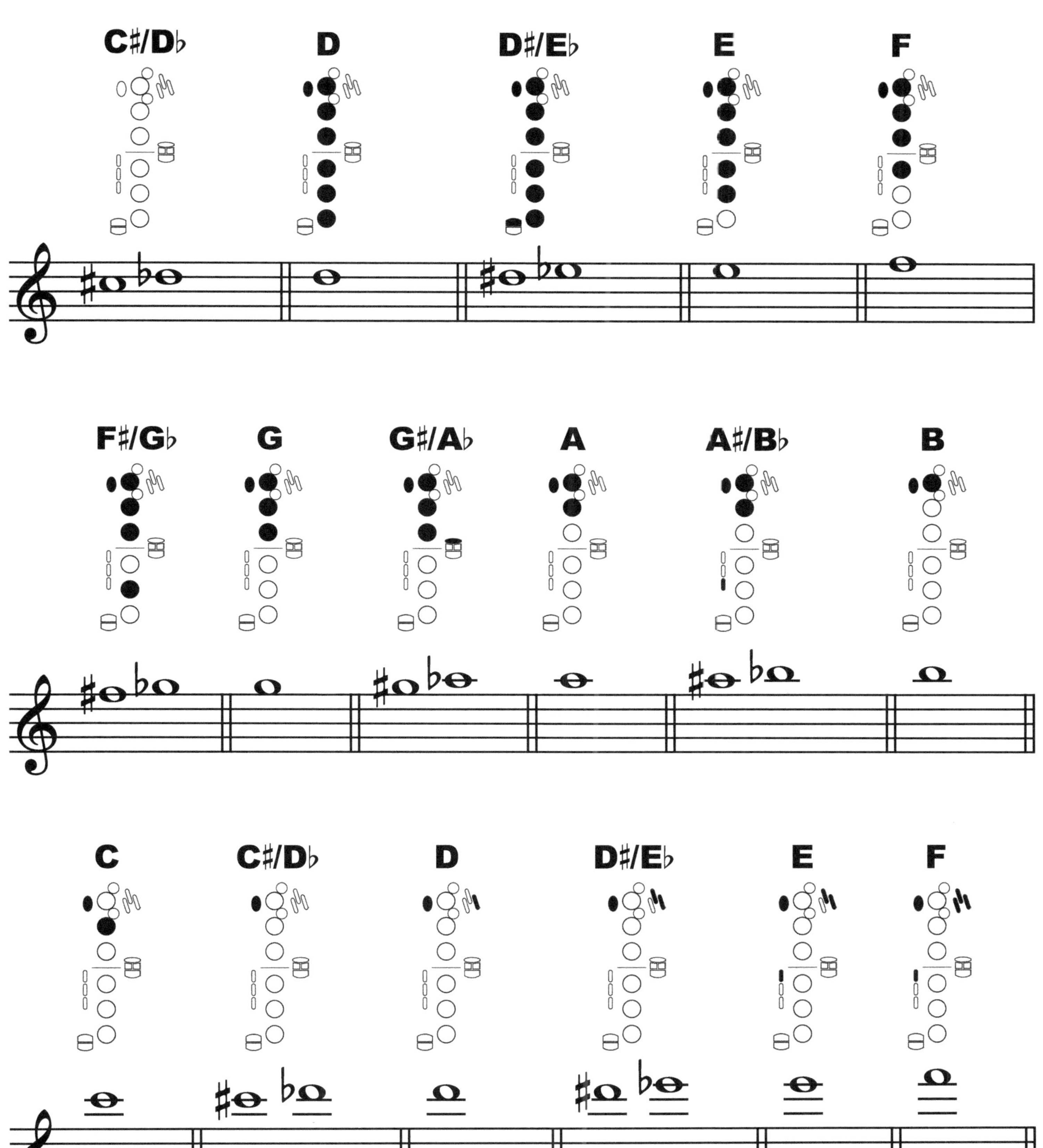
C♯/D♭
D
D♯/E♭
E
F
F♯/G♭
G
G♯/A♭
A
A♯/B♭
B
C
C♯/D♭
D
D♯/E♭
E
F

WEEK 1: C MAJOR

MONDAY: LONG TONES 1

It's Day 1, so let's get started! On Mondays, you'll get used to doing long tones. *Long tones* are an essential part of any saxophone practice routine; they help develop your embouchure control. By consistently practicing long tones, your tone and intonation will improve greatly over time. Today, you will play the C major scale in long tones. Take a deep breath before each note and then sustain the note for the duration of your breath. Listen to the accompanying audio track. Don't worry if you can't hold the note as long as the track. If you can hold it longer, great.

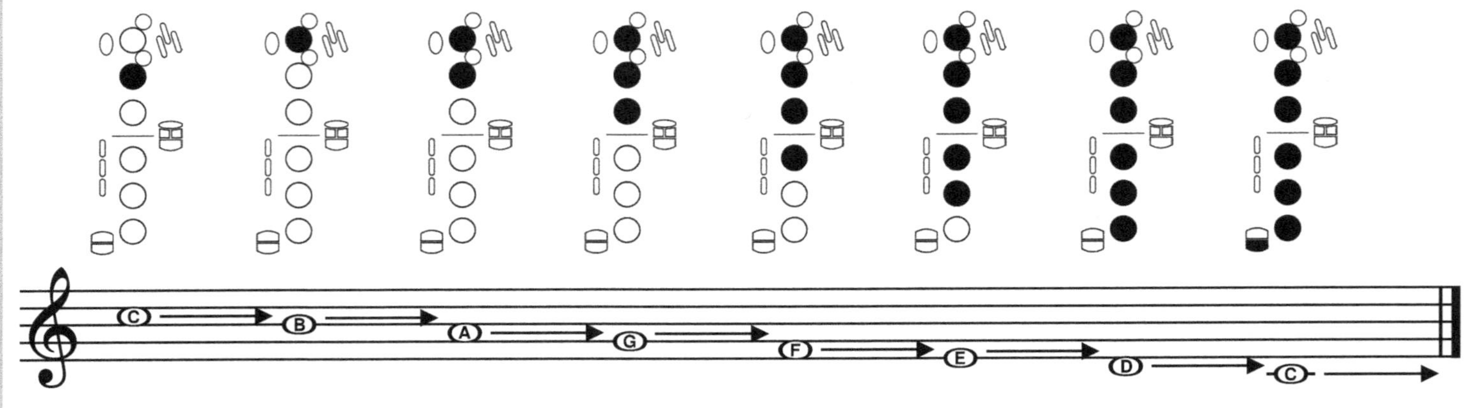

TUESDAY: RHYTHM 2

Tuesdays will focus primarily on rhythm. This first week, you'll start with half notes and whole notes. *Half notes* get two beats, and *whole notes* get four beats. Please use the accompanying audio for any help you might need with the rhythms.

WEDNESDAY: DYNAMICS 3

For the first several weeks, Wednesdays will focus on dynamics. This first week, you will work on *forte* (loud) and *piano* (soft) dynamics.

THURSDAY: TECHNIQUE 4

In the beginning of this book, Thursdays will be dedicated to technique. Focus on moving all your fingers at precisely the same time when switching notes. The technique exercises will get progressively more difficult. Please practice them as many times as needed to master the technique. Start slowly and gradually speed up as you get more comfortable with each exercise.

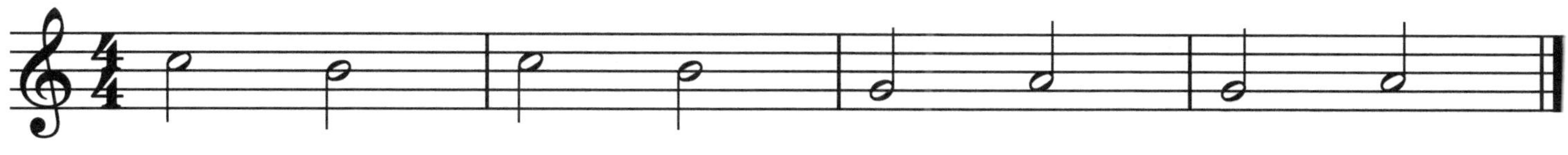

FRIDAY: INTERVALS 5

On Fridays, you'll work on intervals. Today, you'll practice the C major scale in 3rds.

SATURDAY: ORNAMENTATION 6

Ornamentation is the subject on Saturdays. This week, you'll start working on trills. A *trill* is an ornamentation whereby you move back-and-forth from the written note to the note above it within the key signature. Most trills use the normal fingerings; however some trills use special fingerings due to the difficult nature of quickly moving from one note to another. Please use the trill chart (page 5) to check for special fingerings.

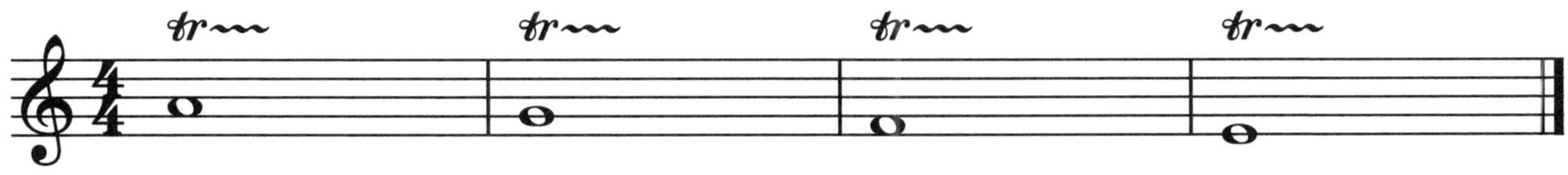

SUNDAY: MUSICAL PIECE 7

A new musical piece is presented each Sunday. These pieces will include topics covered during the week. Just like everything in this book, the musical pieces will increase in difficulty as you go on.

WEEK 2: F MAJOR

MONDAY: LONG TONES 8

You made it to Week 2! This week, you'll work on the F major scale. Take your time with the long tones. Stay relaxed as you take deep breaths and keep the tone of the note as steady as possible as you exhale.

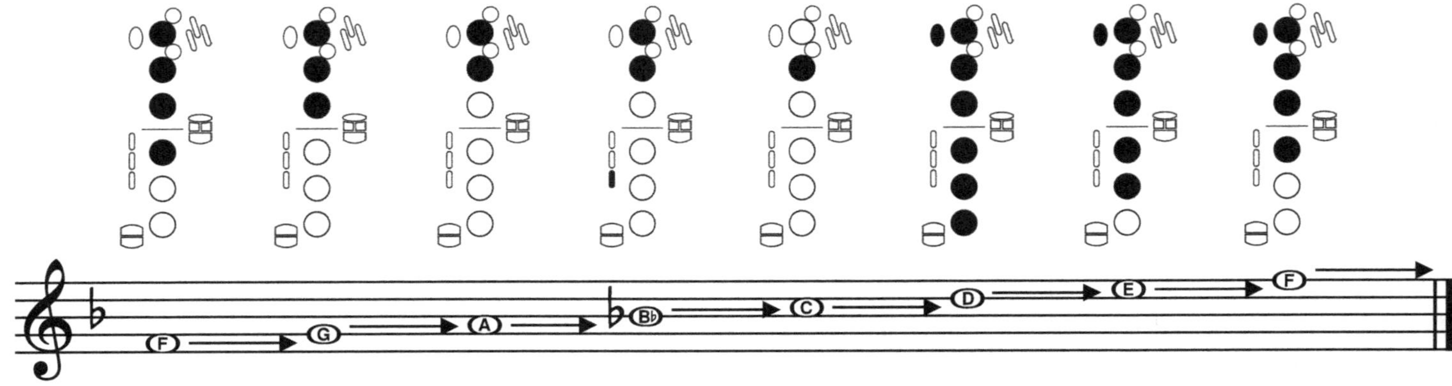

TUESDAY: RHYTHM 9

Here is an exercise that uses the F major scale to work on half notes and whole notes.

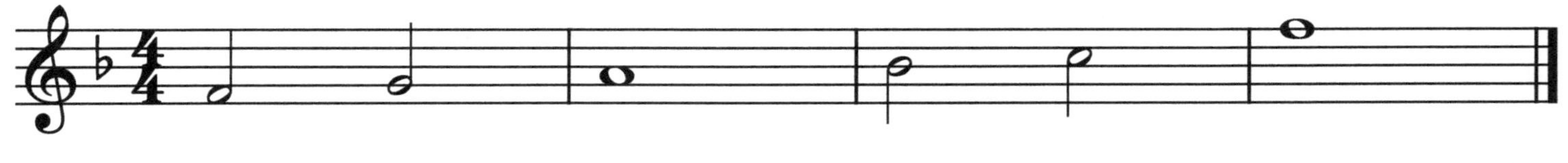

WEDNESDAY: DYNAMICS 10

Follow the dynamics carefully in this exercise.

THURSDAY: TECHNIQUE 11

In this technique exercise, focus on switching from B♭ to C. This can be a difficult transition sometimes. Make sure that all your fingers are moving together.

FRIDAY: INTERVALS 12

Here is the F major scale descending in 3rds.

SATURDAY: ORNAMENTATION 13

Before you start practicing, check for special fingerings for these trills in the trill chart on page 5.

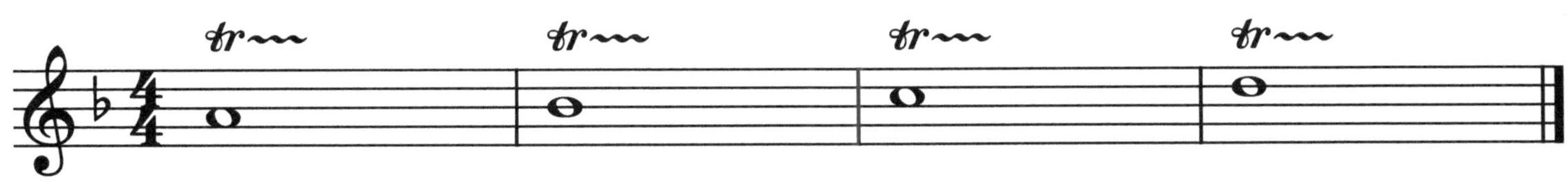

SUNDAY: MUSICAL PIECE 14

This musical piece incorporates dynamics, trills, and rhythm.

WEEK 3: G MAJOR

MONDAY: LONG TONES 15

This week, you'll be working on the G major scale. Start with some long tones to get used to the notes. If you have extra time, play the notes of the scale in ascending fashion, as well.

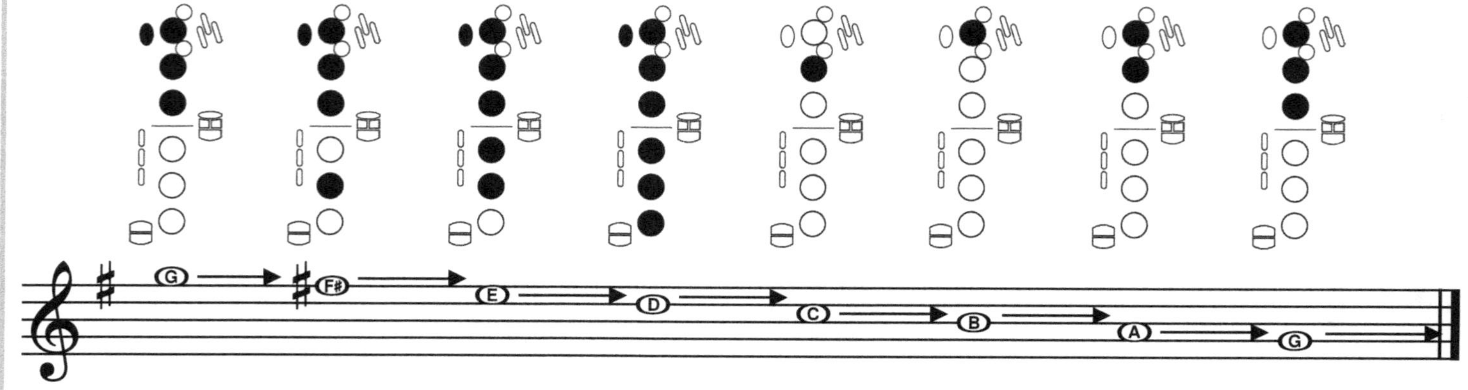

TUESDAY: RHYTHM 16

Today, you'll add quarter notes to your rhythm studies. Quarter notes get one beat.

WEDNESDAY: DYNAMICS 17

For Day 17, you'll add a new dynamic, *mp*, or *mezzo piano*, which means "moderately soft."

THURSDAY: TECHNIQUE 18

While working on the following technique exercise, try to keep the rhythm of the notes perfectly even. Start slow and gradually work your way up in tempo as you practice.

FRIDAY: INTERVALS 19

Let's ascend the G major scale in 3rds today.

SATURDAY: ORNAMENTATION 20

Please practice these trills individually before playing the exercise all together.

SUNDAY: MUSICAL PIECE 21

Things are starting to get a little more challenging now. For this week's musical piece, you'll have to think about dynamics, rhythm, notes, and trills all at the same time.

WEEK 4: B♭ MAJOR

MONDAY: LONG TONES 22

This week, you'll work with the B♭ major scale. Play long tones of the scale as written and also in the lower octave if you have time.

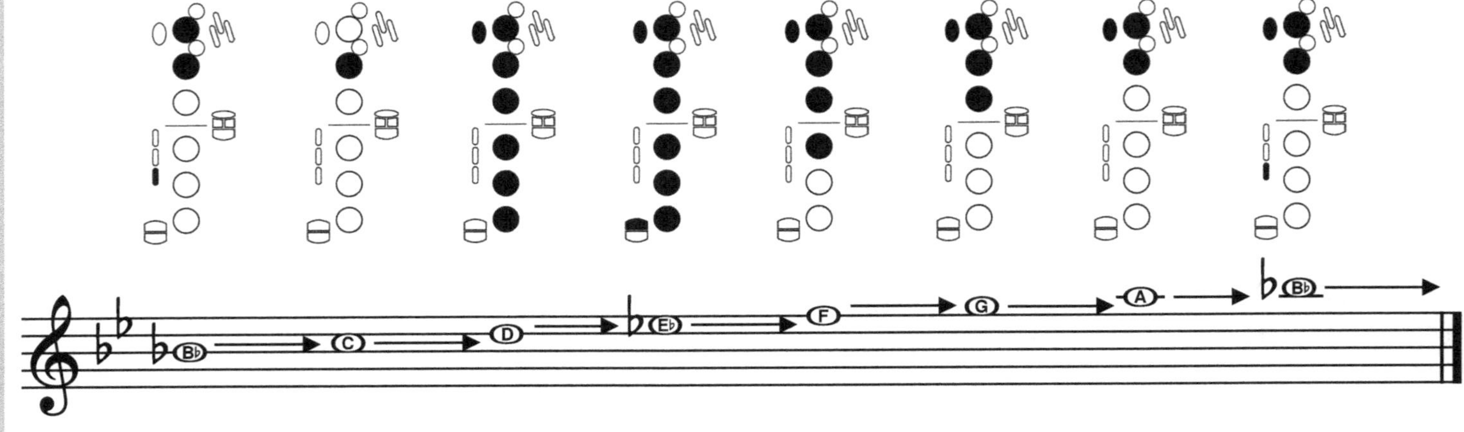

TUESDAY: RHYTHM 23

You'll spend one more week working with whole notes, half notes, and quarter notes before we start to add rests to the rhythm practices on Tuesdays.

WEDNESDAY: DYNAMICS 24

Try to make a big dynamic contrast between the *forte* in the first two bars and the *piano* in the second two bars of the following exercise.

THURSDAY: TECHNIQUE 25

Here is a technique exercise using all quarter notes and the B♭ major scale.

FRIDAY: INTERVALS 26

Start slowly on the next exercise, which goes down the B♭ major scale in 3rds. Concentrate on intonation and precision of fingerings.

SATURDAY: ORNAMENTATION 27

There are a lot of trills in the following exercise, so please look at each one individually and check the trill fingering chart to make sure you're using the proper fingerings.

SUNDAY: MUSICAL PIECE 28

Here is your musical piece for the end of Week 4. Congratulations on getting this far! Keep up the good work! Consistency is the key. When using trills in a musical piece, they usually start from the upper note. Listen to the recorded example and start the trills from the upper note.

WEEK 5: D MAJOR

MONDAY: LONG TONES — 29

This week, you'll work on the D major scale. Here is the D major scale in long tones:

D C# B A G F# E D

TUESDAY: RHYTHM — 30

Today, you'll add quarter-note rests and half-note rests to your rhythm exercise.

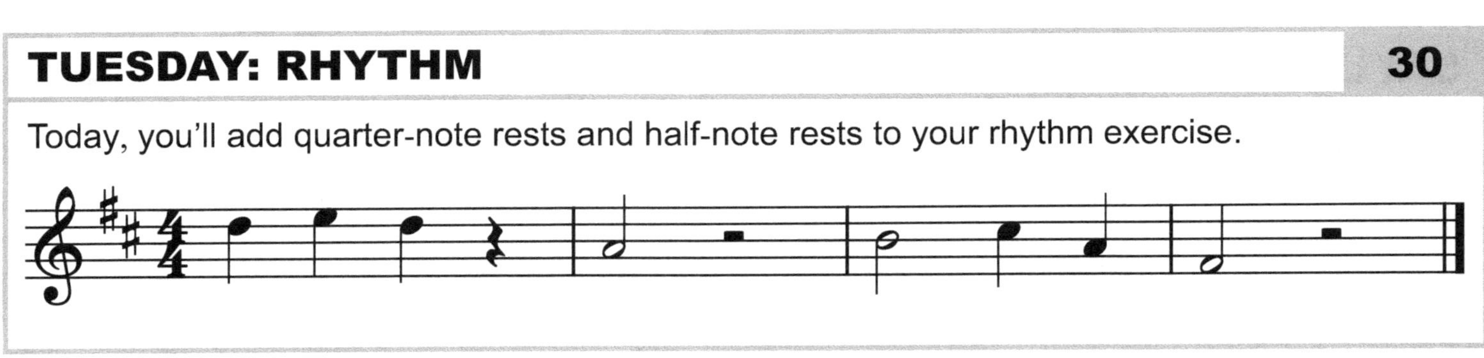

WEDNESDAY: DYNAMICS — 31

The symbol *mp* stands for *mezzo piano*, which means "moderately quiet." We will use this dynamic in today's exercise.

THURSDAY: TECHNIQUE 32

For the next several weeks, you'll be playing scales in groups of four notes to work on technique. Here is the D major scale going down in groups of 4:

FRIDAY: INTERVALS 33

Here, you'll increase the interval between notes to a 4th. Try to hear the pitch of the next note before you play it so that you can stay in tune.

SATURDAY: ORNAMENTATION 34

In today's exercise, C♯ is the only note that requires a special trill fingering. Make sure you check the trill chart.

SUNDAY: MUSICAL PIECE 35

Today's musical piece gets a little tricky. Make sure you are increasing the volume with each dynamic change and watch out for that quarter-note rest!

WEEK 6: E♭ MAJOR

MONDAY: LONG TONES 36

The E♭ major scale has three flats. Here is the scale in long tones:

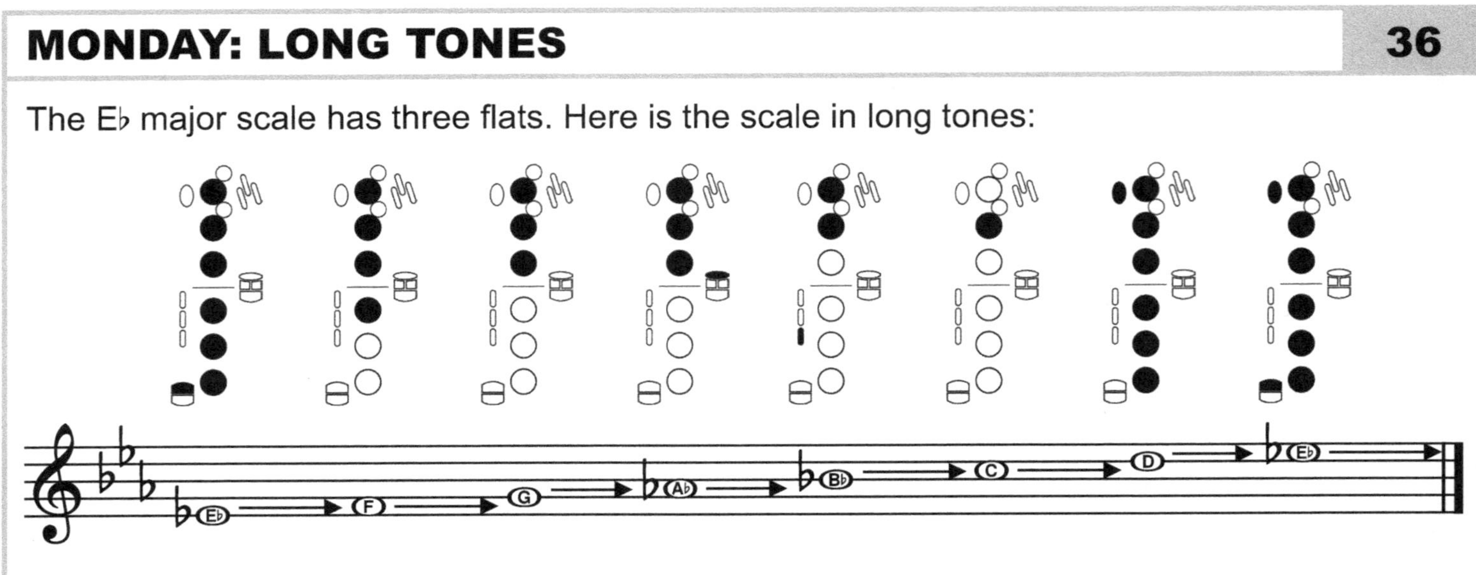

TUESDAY: RHYTHM 37

For Tuesday's rhythm exercise, you will add whole-note rests, which get four beats.

WEDNESDAY: DYNAMICS 38

In this exercise focusing on dynamics, make sure the volume is decreasing with each dynamic marking.

THURSDAY: TECHNIQUE 39

Here is the E♭ major scale ascending in groups of 4.

FRIDAY: INTERVALS 40

For today's interval practice, you'll descend in 4ths through the E♭ major scale.

SATURDAY: ORNAMENTATION 41

Several of the trills in today's exercise have special fingerings, so please start by referencing the trill chart at the beginning of the book.

SUNDAY: MUSICAL PIECE 42

There is a lot to concentrate on in this musical piece. Take your time and start the trills from the higher note.

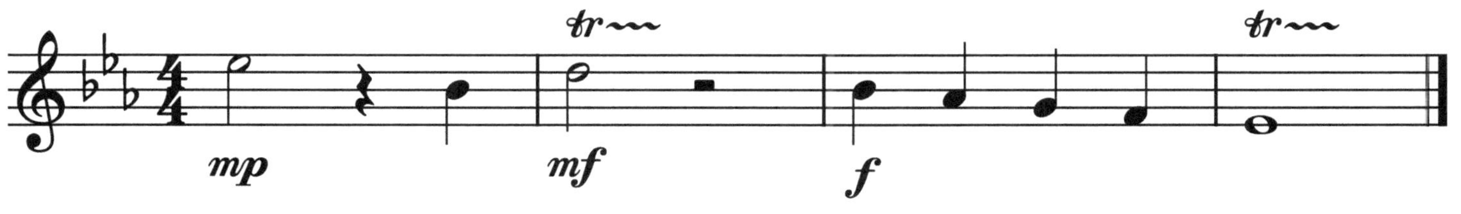

WEEK 7: A MAJOR

MONDAY: LONG TONES 43

Week 7 features the A major scale. Here is the A major scale going down in long tones:

TUESDAY: RHYTHM 44

Before we add eighth notes, we'll work on the same rhythms for the next few weeks. Be careful counting the rests.

WEDNESDAY: DYNAMICS 45

Today, you'll start working on gradual dynamic changes. In this exercise, you'll find a *crescendo*. One way of marking a crescendo is with the hairpin symbol found in this exercise. The hairpin symbol means to gradually increase the volume for the duration of the symbol.

THURSDAY: TECHNIQUE 46

In the following exercise, you will ascend the A major scale in groups of three notes.

FRIDAY: INTERVALS 47

For today's interval practice, you'll go up the scale in 4ths.

SATURDAY: ORNAMENTATION 48

Today, you'll start working on vibrato. *Vibrato* is a slight fluctuation in pitch. This fluctuation in pitch is achieved through very minor changes in the pressure placed on the reed by your embouchure. This is meant to add a desired warmth and rich quality to your sound. Normally, vibrato is not notated and is instead left to the discretion of the player. In the first few weeks, while you're working on vibrato, I will notate it with a wavy line above the staff. This is just to remind you to add vibrato. Once you get used to it, you'll add vibrato almost all the time—it will just become a natural part of your playing. The rate and depth of your vibrato depend on the context of the music you're playing.

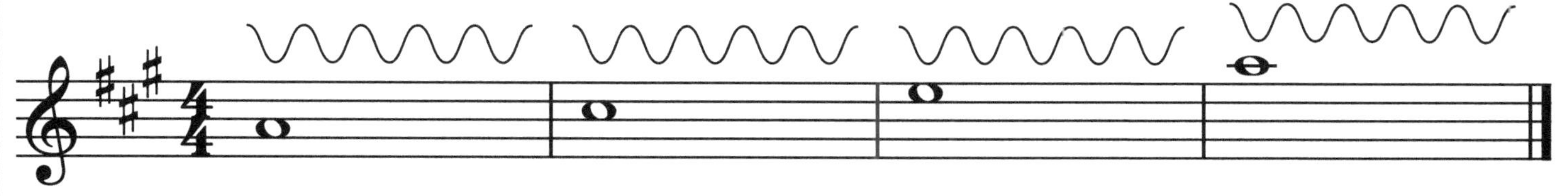

SUNDAY: MUSICAL PIECE 49

There are a lot of dynamics in the following musical piece, so please follow them carefully. I have notated vibrato for the longer-held notes.

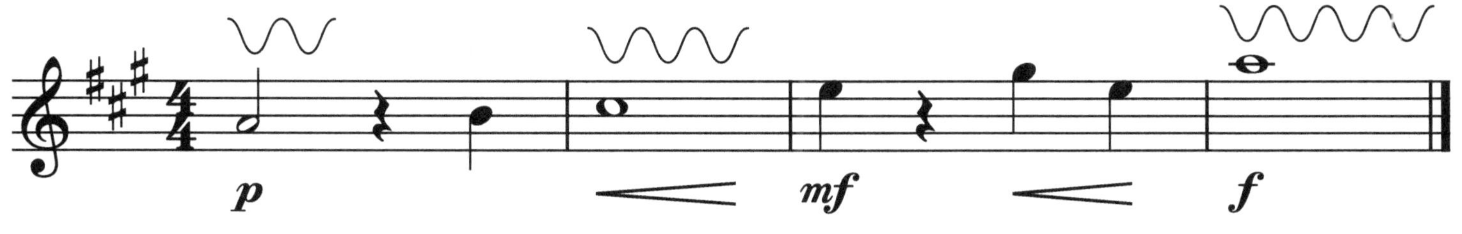

WEEK 8: A♭ MAJOR

MONDAY: LONG TONES 50

This week is the A♭ major scale. Pay attention to the key signatures as we add more sharps and flats each week.

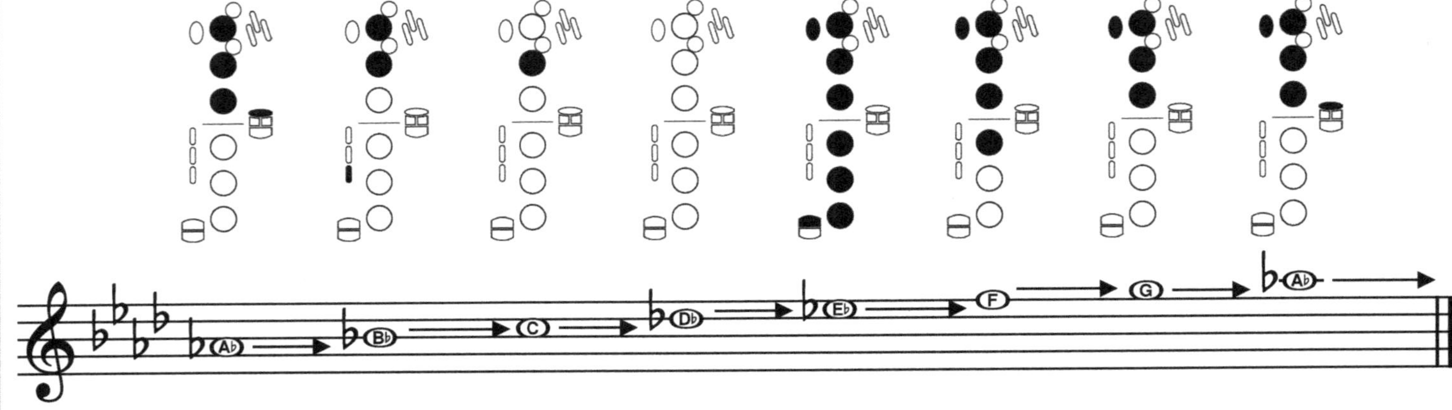

TUESDAY: RHYTHM 51

I'm starting to mix up the rhythms a little bit to give you more of a challenge. Make sure you count and use a metronome if you have one.

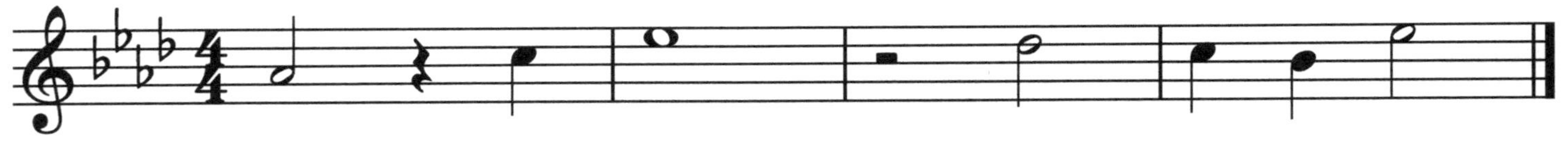

WEDNESDAY: DYNAMICS 52

Today's exercise has a relatively long crescendo. Make sure you pace yourself so you don't increase the volume too fast on the two whole notes.

THURSDAY: TECHNIQUE 53

Here is the A♭ major scale going down in groups of three notes.

FRIDAY: INTERVALS 54

Today's interval workout consists of descending 4ths.

SATURDAY: ORNAMENTATION 55

Here is your vibrato exercise for the week. Different styles of music use different types of vibrato. In this section of the book, you are using the style of vibrato generally associated with classical music, which keeps a pretty consistent depth and rate. In other styles of music, like jazz, the vibrato can change throughout the course of a note.

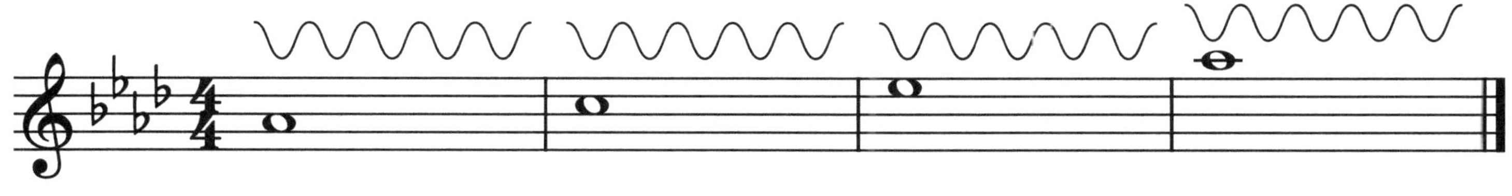

SUNDAY: MUSICAL PIECE 56

Here is the musical piece for this week!

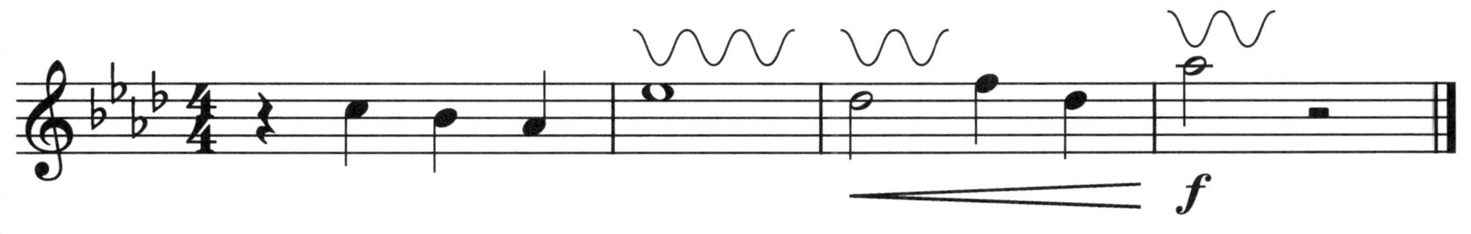

WEEK 9: E MAJOR

MONDAY: LONG TONES 57

The E major scale has four sharps. Here is your long-tone exercise to start Week 9:

TUESDAY: RHYTHM 58

Look closely at today's rhythm exercise before starting to work on it. This piece has rests at the beginning of some measures.

WEDNESDAY: DYNAMICS 59

Each whole note in the following exercise increases in volume, but only to the level of the next dynamic marking.

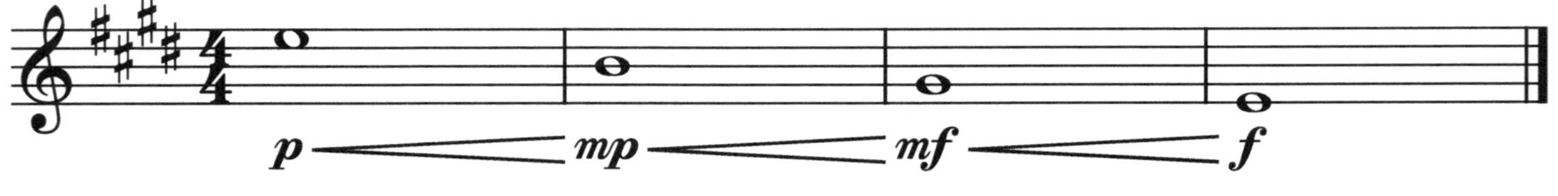

THURSDAY: TECHNIQUE 60

Repetition is a great technique to help achieve synchronization of your fingers when switching between notes on the saxophone. Here, you repeat the same interval a couple of times before switching to the next.

FRIDAY: INTERVALS 61

This week, you'll work on 5ths. As the intervals get wider, it's more difficult to maintain proper intonation at the beginning of each note. Therefore, it's essential that you imagine the pitch of the note you're about to play before going to it. This is a technique that you'll get used to, if you are not already, when playing wide intervals on the saxophone.

SATURDAY: ORNAMENTATION 62

You'll notice that the rate/speed of the vibrato stays pretty consistent on the recordings accompanying these vibrato exercises. However, when you're practicing them, you should try to vary the rate/speed of the vibrato so you can gain better control of it.

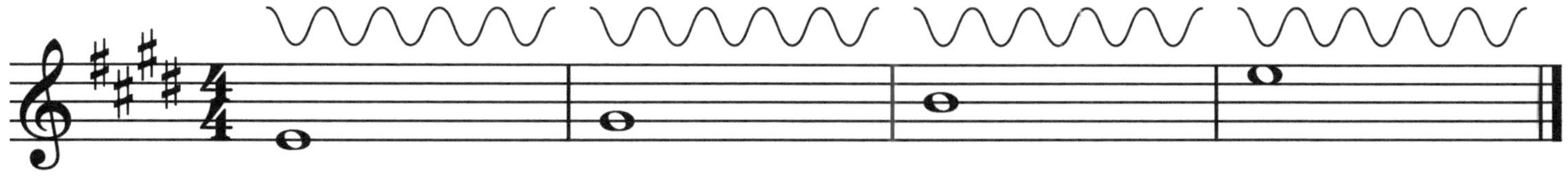

SUNDAY: MUSICAL PIECE 63

In today's musical piece, there is no notation for vibrato. As I mentioned earlier in the book, vibrato is not normally notated but is usually expected. Listen to the recorded example and add vibrato to the longer-held notes in this musical piece.

WEEK 10: D♭ MAJOR

MONDAY: LONG TONES 64

Hopefully, you're starting to enjoy practicing long tones. They can be relaxing and meditative. Here is the D♭ major scale in long tones:

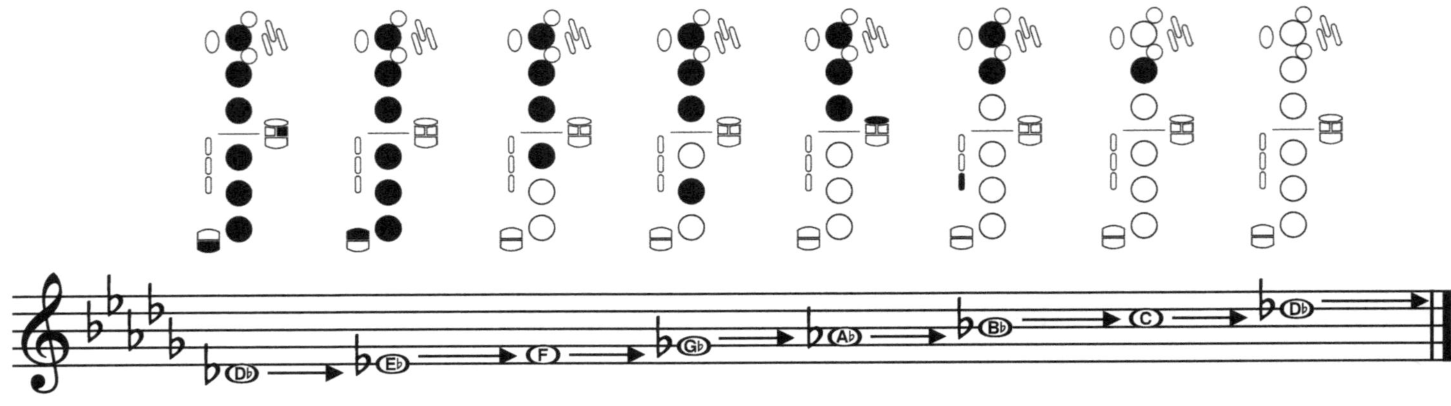

TUESDAY: RHYTHM 65

Here is the rhythm exercise for this week:

WEDNESDAY: DYNAMICS 66

The following exercise introduces the *decrescendo*. One method for notating a decrescendo is with a hairpin marking. Get gradually quieter for the duration of the marking.

THURSDAY: TECHNIQUE — 67

In today's technique exercise, you'll be playing repeated 3rds that descend through the D♭ major scale.

FRIDAY: INTERVALS — 68

This week, you'll continue to work on 5ths. Here is the D♭ major scale descending in 5ths:

SATURDAY: ORNAMENTATION — 69

Here is the D♭ major scale ascending in 5ths, with markings to remind you to add vibrato:

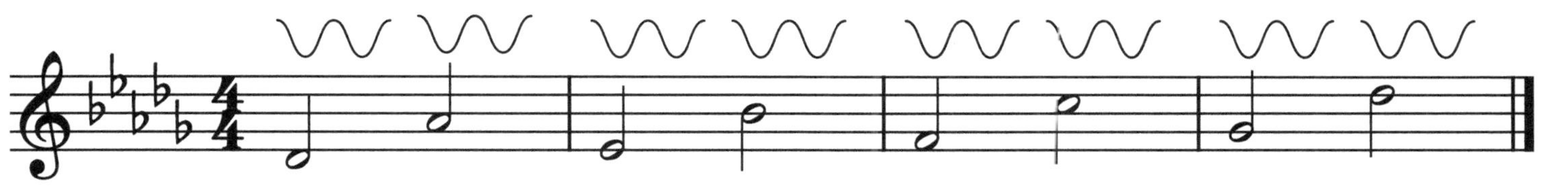

SUNDAY: MUSICAL PIECE — 70

This musical piece incorporates material you have learned so far in the book. Don't forget to add vibrato to the longer notes.

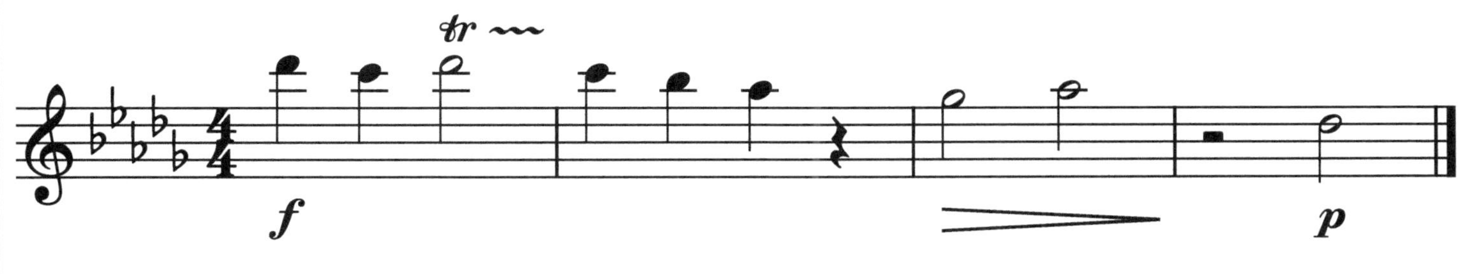

WEEK 11: B MAJOR

MONDAY: LONG TONES 71

This week, you'll work on the B major scale.

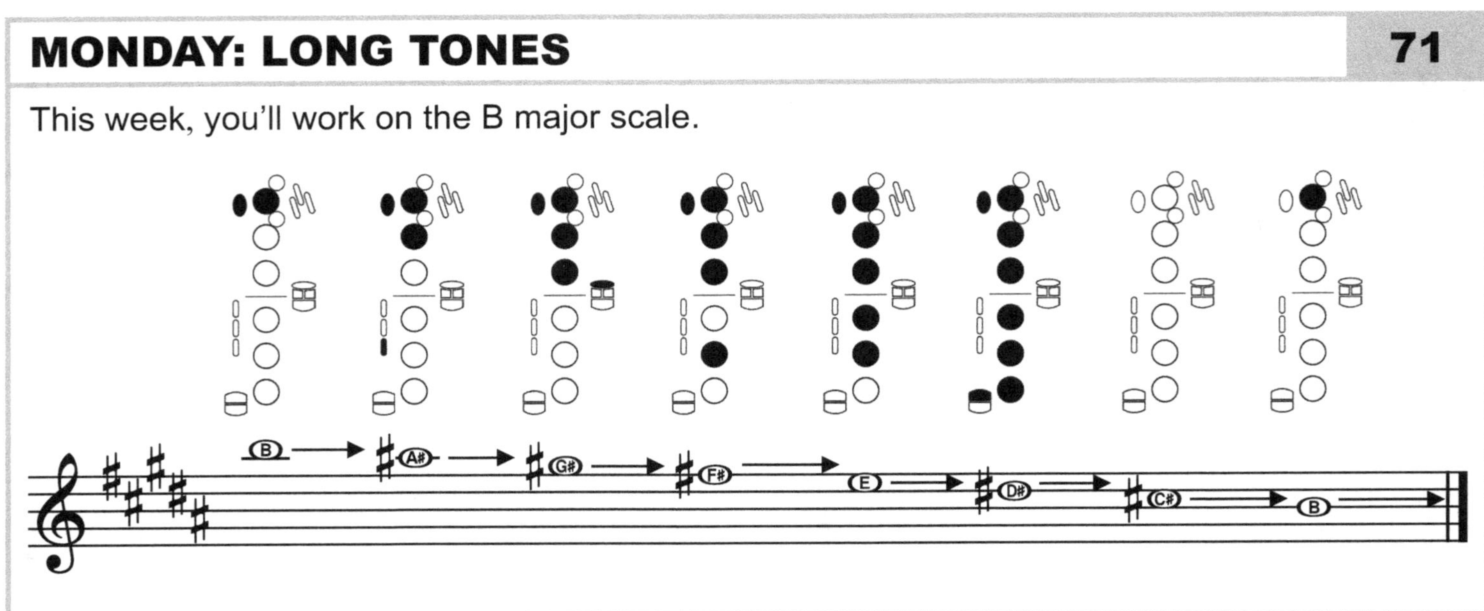

TUESDAY: RHYTHM 72

Here is your rhythm exercise for the week:

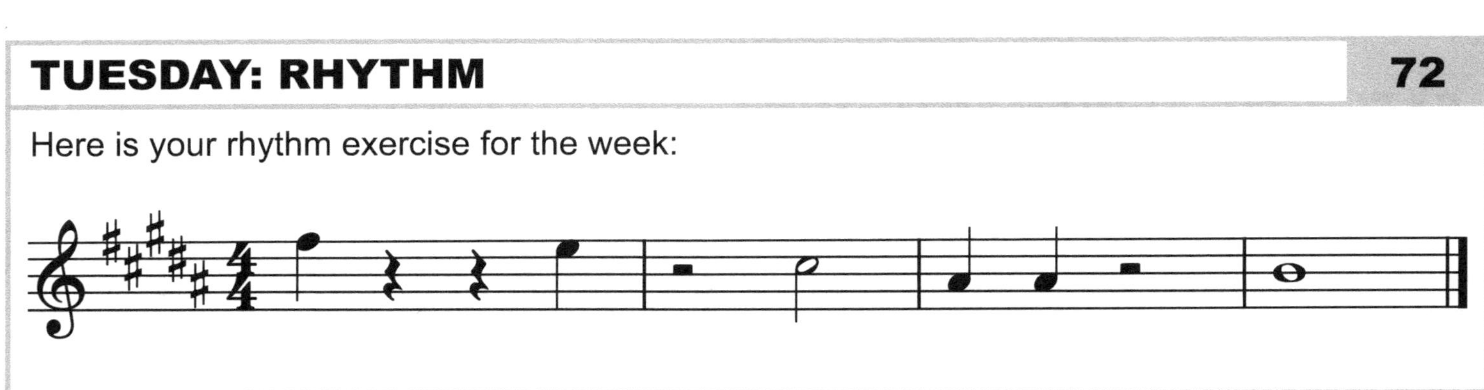

WEDNESDAY: DYNAMICS 73

In today's exercise, you'll encounter a crescendo and a decrescendo. Try to pace yourself so that you arrive at the desired dynamic by the end of the crescendo and decrescendo.

mp *f* *mp*

THURSDAY: TECHNIQUE 74

For today's technique exercise, you'll play repeated 4ths up the B major scale.

FRIDAY: INTERVALS 75

Today, you'll expand your intervals to 6ths. These are very wide and difficult, so take your time and make sure that the pitch of each note is in tune.

SATURDAY: ORNAMENTATION 76

Here is your vibrato exercise for the week. Hopefully, your vibrato is getting steadier and easier to control each week.

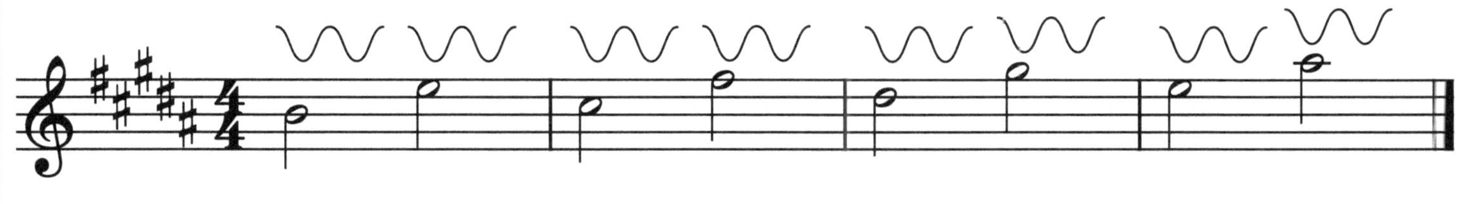

SUNDAY: MUSICAL PIECE 77

Follow the rhythms and dynamics carefully in today's musical piece!

WEEK 12: F♯ MAJOR

MONDAY: LONG TONES 78

Here is the F♯ major scale in long tones. Every note, except for B, is "sharped" in this scale.

TUESDAY: RHYTHM 79

Have fun with this rhythm exercise!

WEDNESDAY: DYNAMICS 80

In the following exercise, you'll bring the volume down with the decrescendo and then back up toward the end with the crescendo.

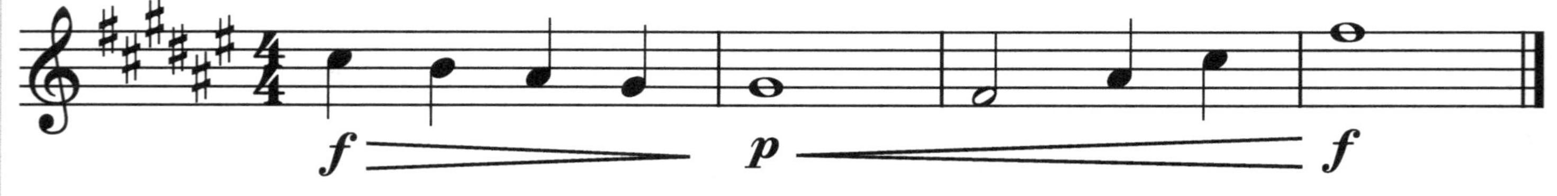

THURSDAY: TECHNIQUE 81

Focus on keeping your fingers close to the keys during this exercise.

FRIDAY: INTERVALS 82

Here is another challenging exercise in 6ths:

SATURDAY: ORNAMENTATION 83

This is your last day of working on vibrato. From now on, use the appropriate vibrato for the style of music that you're playing.

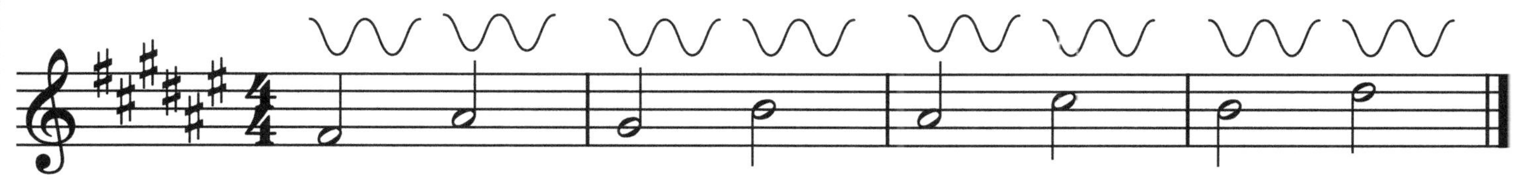

SUNDAY: MUSICAL PIECE 84

Let's wrap up Week 12 with a fun little piece! Next week will be a review week with several musical pieces.

WEEK 13: REVIEW 1

MONDAY: LONG TONES 85

This week consists of review pieces in some of the keys that you worked on so far in the book. First, here is a section of the chromatic scale in long tones for you to work on today:

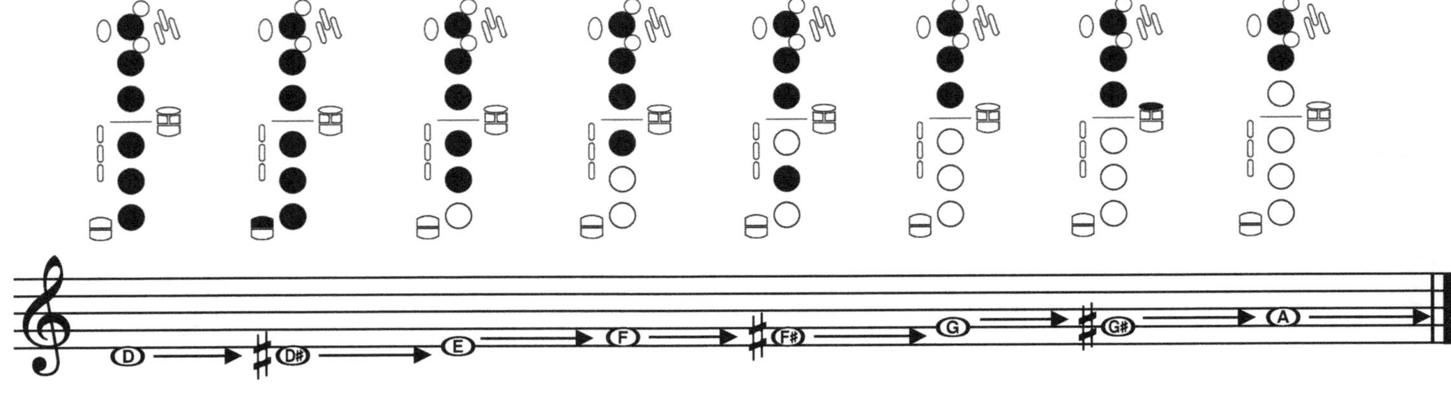

TUESDAY: RHYTHM 86

Here is a piece using the G major scale and focusing on some of the rhythms you have worked on in this book:

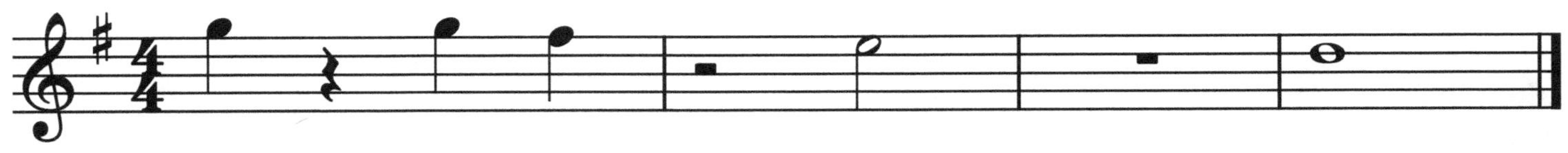

WEDNESDAY: DYNAMICS 87

In this piece, you'll review the F major scale and some dynamic markings.

THURSDAY: TECHNIQUE **88**

Here is a piece using the D major scale:

FRIDAY: INTERVALS **89**

In this piece, you will play a variety of intervals from the B♭ major scale.

SATURDAY: ORNAMENTATION **90**

This piece is a review of trills and vibrato.

SUNDAY: MUSICAL PIECE **91**

For the last day of this review week, you'll play a longer piece incorporating everything you have worked on so far.

WEEK 14: C NATURAL MINOR

MONDAY: LONG TONES 92

In this section of the book, you'll be working on natural minor scales. The *natural minor scale* is a scale built from the sixth note of a major scale. For example, the sixth note of the C major scale is A. If we play the C major scale but start from the note A, we get the A natural minor scale. Therefore, A minor is the *relative minor* of C major, and vice versa. When compared to the major scale sharing the same root note (for example, C major vs C natural minor), the natural minor scale has a lowered 3rd, 6th and 7th note. This week, you'll work on the C natural minor scale (the relative minor of E♭ major) in long tones.

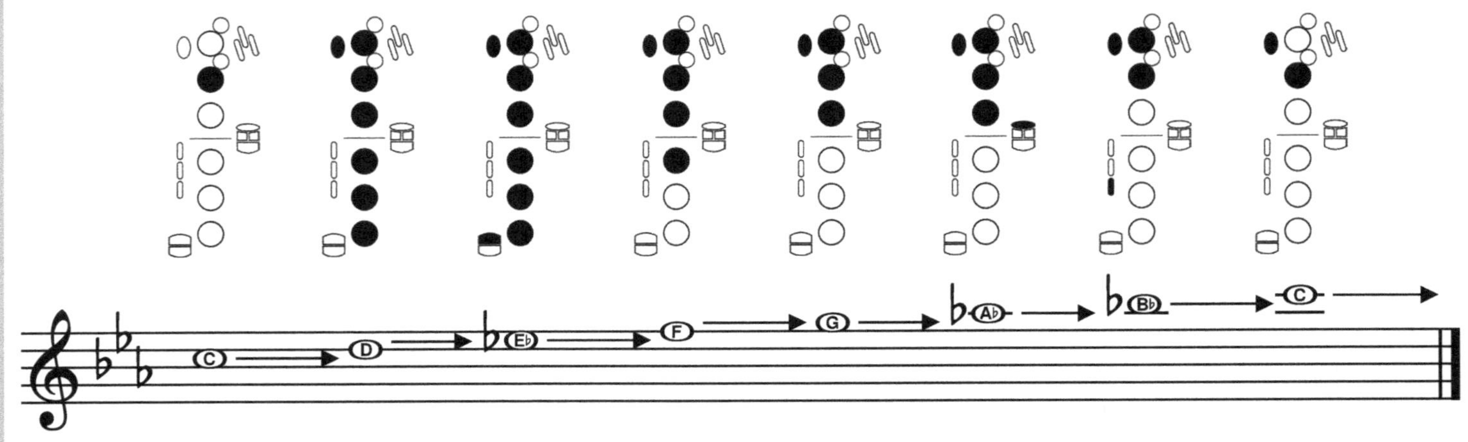

TUESDAY: RHYTHM 93

It's rhythm day! Today, you'll add eighth notes and eighth-note rests. The music should start to become much more interesting in the next few weeks!

WEDNESDAY: ARTICULATION 94

For the next several Wednesdays, you'll be working on different types of articulation. Today's focus is slurs. A *slur* involves keeping the air moving between notes, with no interruption from the tongue. Tongue only the first note under a slur, keeping the air moving for the remaining notes under the slur marking.

THURSDAY: TECHNIQUE 95

Now that you have been introduced to eighth notes, technique day can get much more challenging. Here is an exercise with repeated 2nds ascending the C natural minor scale:

FRIDAY: INTERVALS 96

Keep up the good work! Here is the C natural minor scale in 3rds:

SATURDAY: ORNAMENTATION 97

Today, you'll start working on grace notes. A *grace note* is a type of embellishment that appears as a miniature note preceding a main/normal note. The grace note is usually played quickly, right before the main note. Grace notes require some experience. Depending on the context, grace notes could get more or less value, or more or less emphasis. Please listen to the recorded examples to get an idea of how they should be played.

SUNDAY: MUSICAL PIECE 98

Here is your musical piece for Week 14:

WEEK 15: G NATURAL MINOR

MONDAY: LONG TONES 99

This week, you'll work on the G natural minor scale. Here are your long tones for the week:

G F E♭ D C B♭ A G

TUESDAY: RHYTHM 100

Congratulations on making it through the first 100 days! Here is your rhythm exercise for Week 15:

WEDNESDAY: ARTICULATION 101

Today's musical piece incorporates some slurs. Remember, tongue only the first note under the slur.

THURSDAY: TECHNIQUE 102

This technique exercise uses repeated 3rds to play through the G natural minor scale.

FRIDAY: INTERVALS 103

Listen to the recorded example before practicing this exercise, then try playing along.

SATURDAY: ORNAMENTATION 104

In the next exercise, you'll see many accidentals on the grace notes because each grace note is approaching a note in the G natural minor scale from a half-step below.

SUNDAY: MUSICAL PIECE 105

Today's musical piece is a bit more challenging. Add vibrato, even though it's not notated.

WEEK 16: B♭ NATURAL MINOR

MONDAY: LONG TONES 106

Here is the B♭ natural minor scale in long tones:

TUESDAY: RHYTHM 107

In this rhythm exercise, some of the rests can be tricky, so take your time and count. Try practicing this with a metronome.

WEDNESDAY: ARTICULATION 108

Here is a nice little piece with some slurs:

THURSDAY: TECHNIQUE

109

Some of these fingerings are quite difficult, so start slowly.

FRIDAY: INTERVALS

110

Here is the B♭ natural minor scale in 4ths:

SATURDAY: ORNAMENTATION

111

Listen to the recorded example before playing this exercise with grace notes.

SUNDAY: MUSICAL PIECE

112

Here is your musical piece for Week 16:

WEEK 17: F NATURAL MINOR

MONDAY: LONG TONES 113

Week 17 starts with long tones from the F natural minor scale:

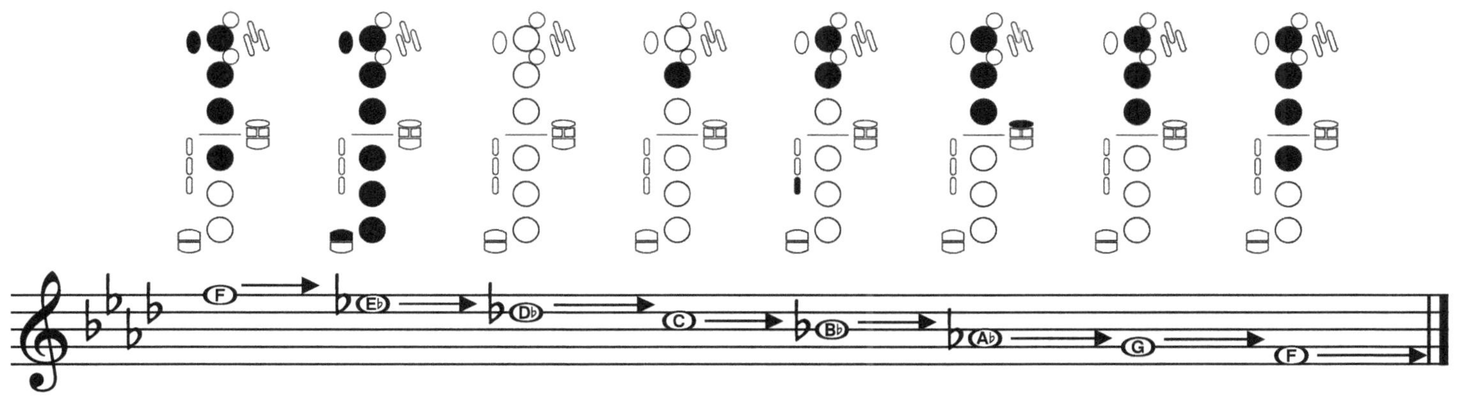

TUESDAY: RHYTHM 114

Today, you'll incorporate dotted quarter notes into your rhythm practice. A dot increases the duration of the note by half of its original rhythmic value. So, a dotted quarter note gets one-and-a-half beats (quarter note = 1 beat, dot = 1/2 beat).

WEDNESDAY: ARTICULATION 115

Let's add ties to your practice. A *tie* is like a slur, except it connects two notes of the *same* pitch—you simply add the values of the two notes together. Ties are used to go across barlines and across the midpoint of a measure.

THURSDAY: TECHNIQUE — 116

Here are some repeated 5ths for you to work on your technique and intonation. Start very slowly with this exercise and increase the tempo as you get more comfortable.

FRIDAY: INTERVALS — 117

Today, you'll work on some intervals with slurs. When slurring a wide interval like a 4th in the following exercise, you'll have to adjust the position of your tongue to achieve proper intonation. You want to use more of an "Oh" tongue formation for the lower notes, and an "ee" formation for the upper notes.

SATURDAY: ORNAMENTATION — 118

The following exercise uses double grace notes.

SUNDAY: MUSICAL PIECE — 119

Here is a musical piece to finish off your week!

WEEK 18: D NATURAL MINOR

MONDAY: LONG TONES 120

The D natural minor scale has only one accidental, B♭. Have fun with the material this week! As the pieces get more advanced, they also get more interesting.

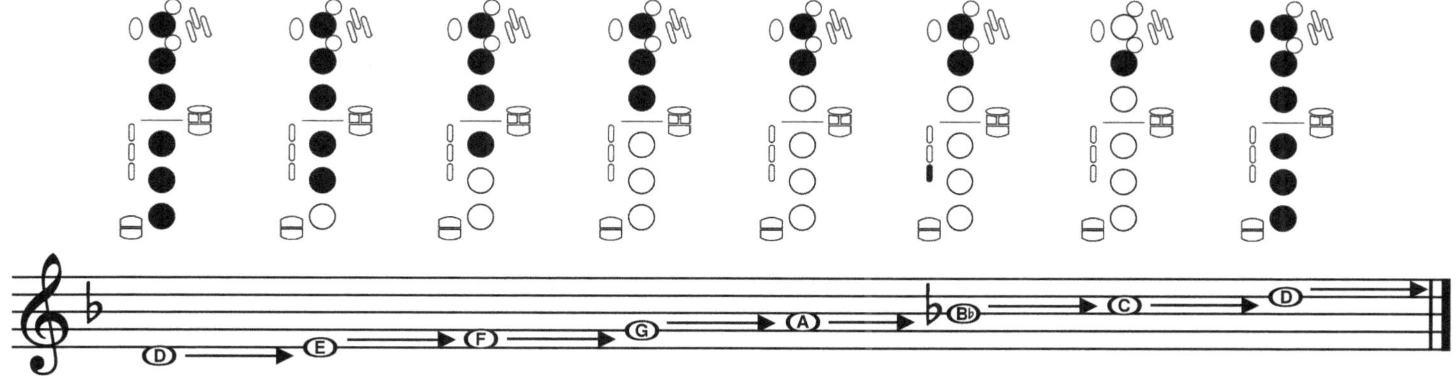

TUESDAY: RHYTHM 121

Here is a rhythm exercise using dotted quarter notes:

WEDNESDAY: ARTICULATION 122

In this exercise, a tie is used to demonstrate the rhythm of a dotted quarter note. The very first note is written as a quarter note tied to an eighth note but could be written as a dotted quarter note like in measure 2.

THURSDAY: TECHNIQUE 123

Here is the D natural minor scale in groups of 3:

FRIDAY: INTERVALS 124

Today is a continuation of the topic from last week: intervals with slurs.

SATURDAY: ORNAMENTATION 125

You would never see this many grace notes in written music—this is simply an exercise. Go over each grace note individually before trying to put them all together. This exercise should take you a little while to master.

SUNDAY: MUSICAL PIECE 126

With all the different things to concentrate on in this musical piece, don't forget the dynamics!

WEEK 19: E♭ NATURAL MINOR

MONDAY: LONG TONES 127

Here is the E♭ natural minor scale in long tones. Some of the accidentals are tricky: C♭ is the same note as B natural, and G♭ is the same as F♯.

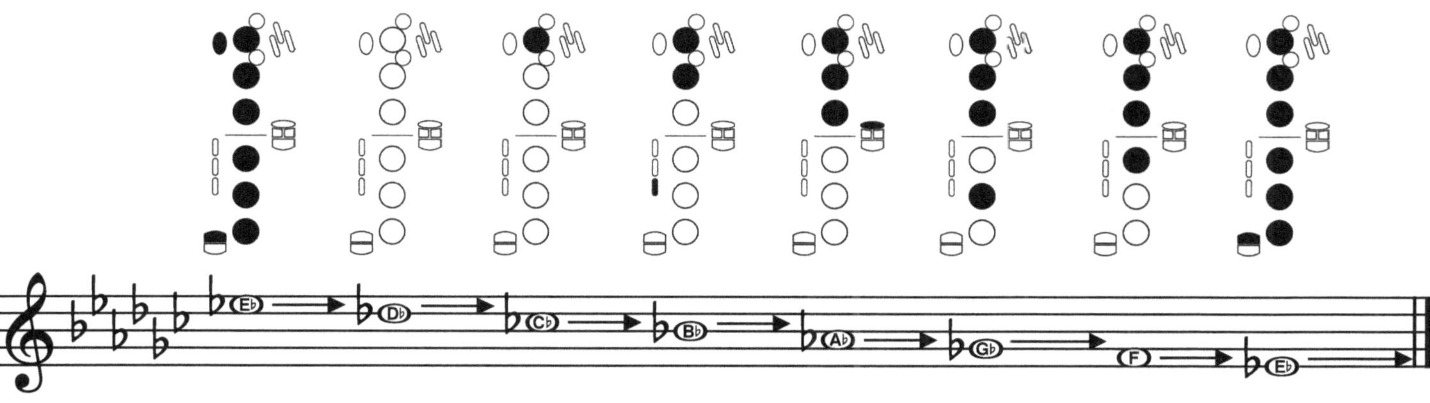

TUESDAY: RHYTHM 128

Today, you'll add dotted half notes to your rhythm practice. A dotted half note gets three beats (half note = 2 beats, dot = 1 beat).

WEDNESDAY: ARTICULATION 129

The next piece has ties, slurs, and a pickup measure. A *pickup measure* is used when the music starts before the first beat of bar 1.

THURSDAY: TECHNIQUE 130

Here is the E♭ natural minor scale in groups of four notes.

FRIDAY: INTERVALS 131

In this piece, you'll play 6ths with slurs.

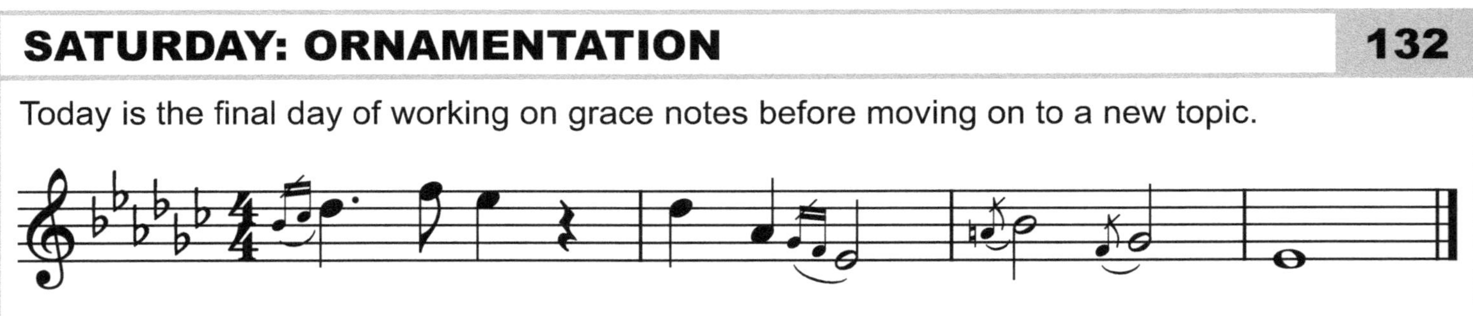

SATURDAY: ORNAMENTATION 132

Today is the final day of working on grace notes before moving on to a new topic.

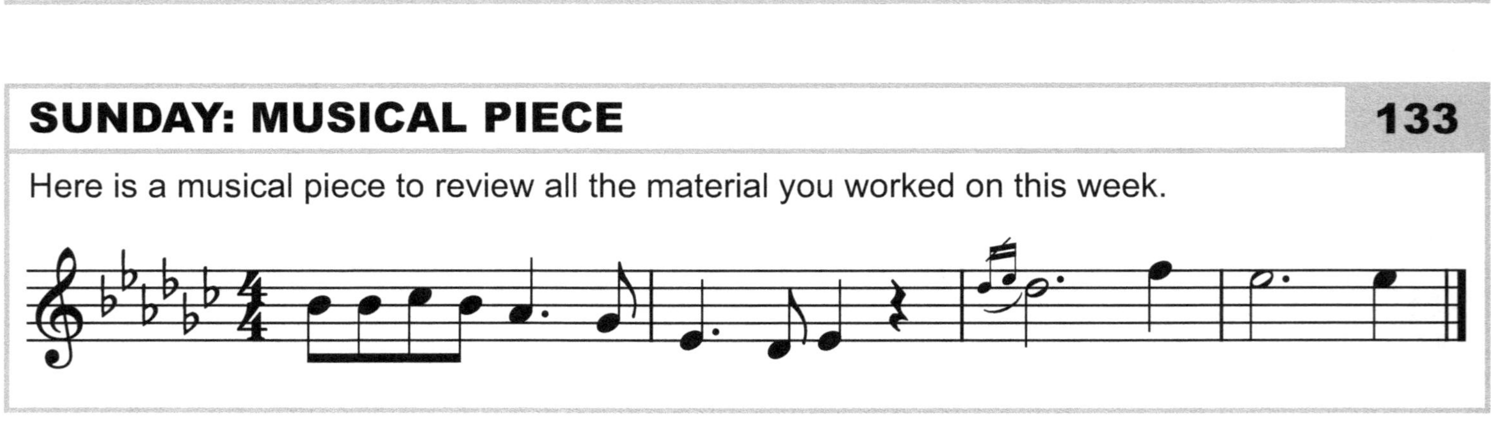

SUNDAY: MUSICAL PIECE 133

Here is a musical piece to review all the material you worked on this week.

WEEK 20: A NATURAL MINOR

MONDAY: LONG TONES — 134

This week features the A natural minor scale. A natural minor is the relative minor scale of C major, so there are no flats or sharps in this scale.

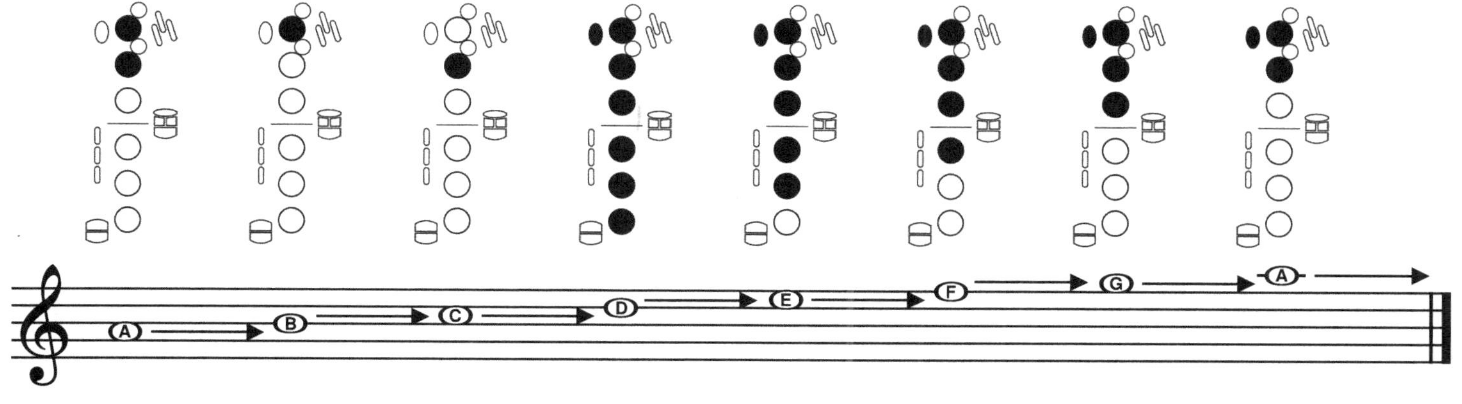

TUESDAY: RHYTHM — 135

The first measure of this rhythm exercise is difficult, so please listen to the recorded example first, and then start to work on this piece.

WEDNESDAY: ARTICULATION — 136

Today, you'll add a new articulation, *staccato*, which is notated with a dot above or below the notehead. Staccato indicates that the note is to be played in a short, separated manner. The length of the note will depend on the context and the tempo of the piece. Listen to the recorded example to get an idea of how to play staccato articulation.

THURSDAY: TECHNIQUE 137

Let's add some articulation to your technique study this week. Here is the A natural minor scale in groups of 4, with slur and staccato articulations added:

FRIDAY: INTERVALS 138

Here is this week's interval workout:

SATURDAY: DYNAMICS 139

Today's musical piece contains a *ritardando* (abbreviated as "rit" in most pieces of music) at the end. This symbol means to gradually slow down for the duration of the ritardando. Listen to the recorded example before starting to work on this piece.

SUNDAY: MUSICAL PIECE 140

Here is a musical piece for you to wrap up the week with. It contains all of the material you worked on this week.

WEEK 21: A♭ NATURAL MINOR

MONDAY: LONG TONES

141

This week's scale, A♭ natural minor, is tricky because every note is flatted. Here is the scale in long tones:

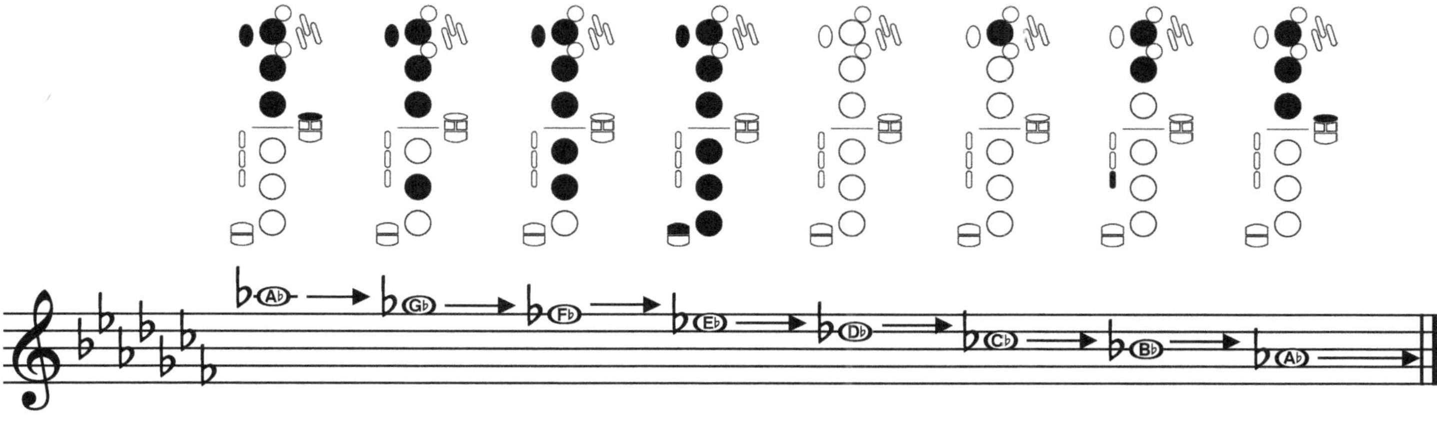

TUESDAY: RHYTHM

142

Here's a nice musical piece highlighting some rhythms that you have worked on. Once again, I'll remind you to regard the key signature.

WEDNESDAY: ARTICULATION

143

The following piece focuses on articulation and there is some nice syncopation in bars 1 and 4.

THURSDAY: TECHNIQUE 144

This is the A♭ natural minor scale going down in groups of 4, with tongue-two/slur-two articulation.

FRIDAY: INTERVALS 145

In this piece, you'll play 6ths intervals with tongue-two/slur-two articulation.

SATURDAY: DYNAMICS 146

In today's piece, you'll find some grace notes and a ritardando at the end.

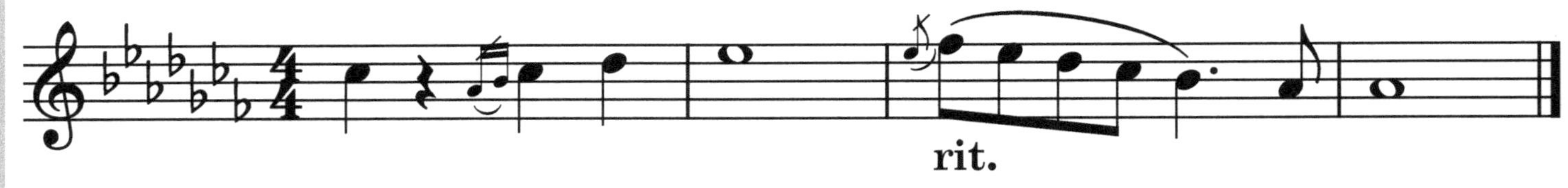

SUNDAY: MUSICAL PIECE 147

There is a lot squeezed into this four-bar musical piece. Take your time while working on this one.

WEEK 22: E NATURAL MINOR

MONDAY: LONG TONES 148

Week 22 should be a bit easier due to having only one sharp to deal with this week, F♯.

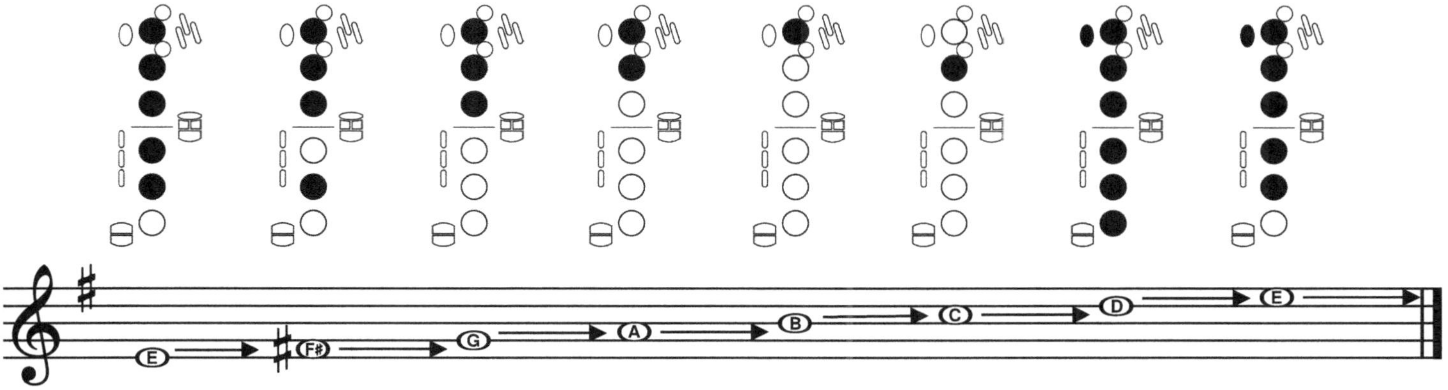

TUESDAY: RHYTHM 149

Tuesday and Wednesday of this week both work on articulation and rhythms. Here's the first exercise:

WEDNESDAY: ARTICULATION 150

Listen to the rhythm and articulation before you try this exercise.

THURSDAY: TECHNIQUE — 151

Today, you'll start working on triads. Here is the E natural minor scale in diatonic triads:

FRIDAY: INTERVALS — 152

This exercise features 7ths intervals. Try to hear the notes in your head before you play them.

SATURDAY: ORNAMENTATION — 153

When you play trills, you almost always start from the above note, although this is not notated in the music. In the following exercise, however, I've placed grace notes coming from the above note as a reminder to start the trill from there.

SUNDAY: MUSICAL PIECE — 154

Here is your musical piece for Week 22. When you listen to the musical example, you'll notice that the trills stop for the added duration of time (i.e., the dot, or half a beat) on the dotted quarter notes. This is a common classical technique for trills.

WEEK 23: C♯ NATURAL MINOR

MONDAY: LONG TONES 155

Here's the C♯ natural minor scale in long tones:

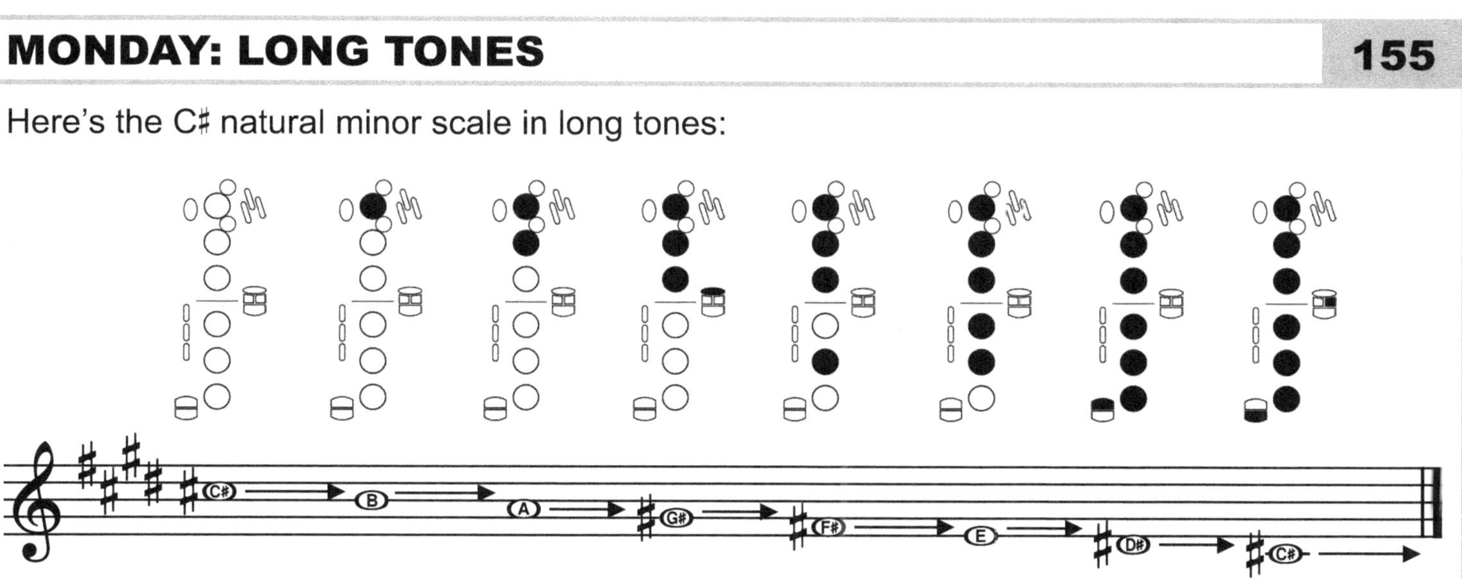

TUESDAY: RHYTHM 156

Today, you'll add 16th notes. This will open up all kinds of fun rhythmic possibilities!

WEDNESDAY: ARTICULATION 157

The following piece contains *tenuto* markings, which direct the performer to sustain the note for the full value and to play it in a smooth and connected manner.

THURSDAY: TECHNIQUE 158

For technique practice, you'll descend the C♯ natural minor scale in triads.

FRIDAY: INTERVALS 159

Here are 7ths going down the C♯ natural minor scale with tenuto and staccato articulations:

SATURDAY: ORNAMENTATION 160

This piece focuses on grace notes and trills (start the trills from the above note).

SUNDAY: MUSICAL PIECE

161

Here is your musical piece for the week. Don't forget to stop the trills for the added time of the dot on the dotted quarter notes.

WEEK 24: B NATURAL MINOR

MONDAY: LONG TONES 162

Here are your long tones for the week. This is the B natural minor scale.

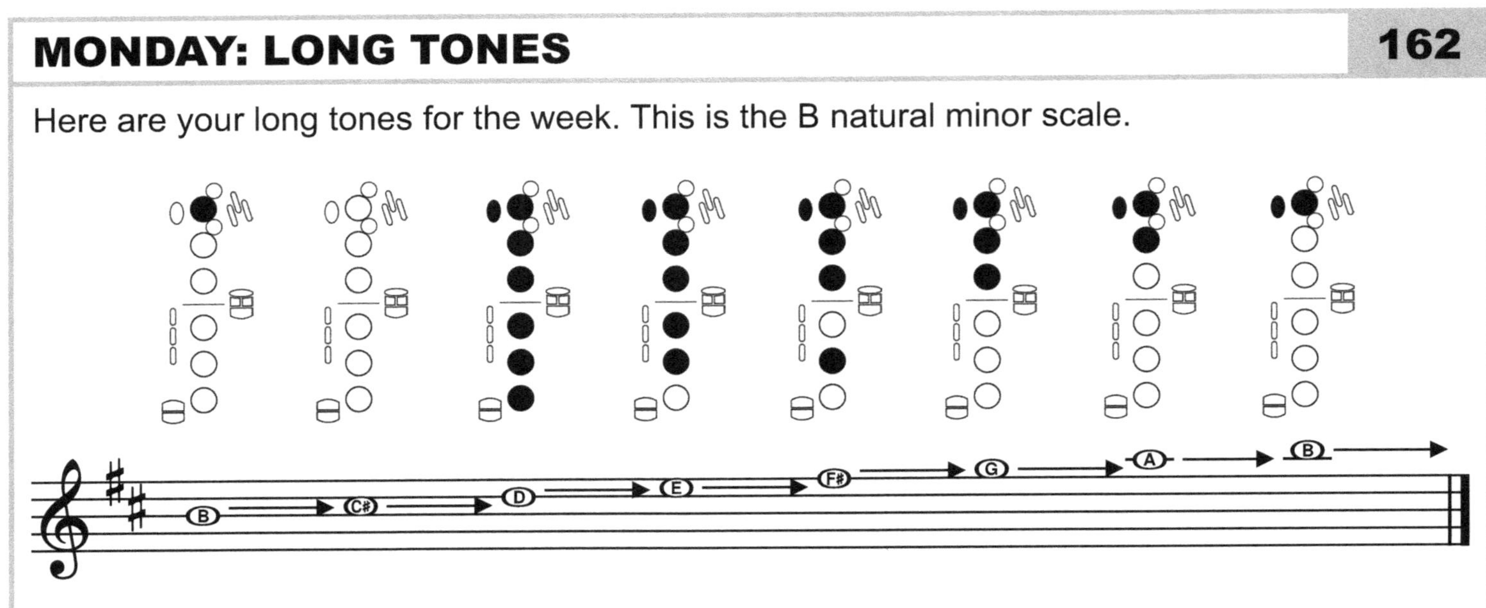

TUESDAY: RHYTHM 163

In this piece, you'll add 16th-note rests. Some of the articulation is difficult. Listen to the recorded example.

WEDNESDAY: ARTICULATION 164

Have fun with this piece!

THURSDAY: TECHNIQUE 165

Here, you'll go through the scale in triads.

FRIDAY: INTERVALS 166

For the next two weeks, you'll play the natural minor scale in octaves.

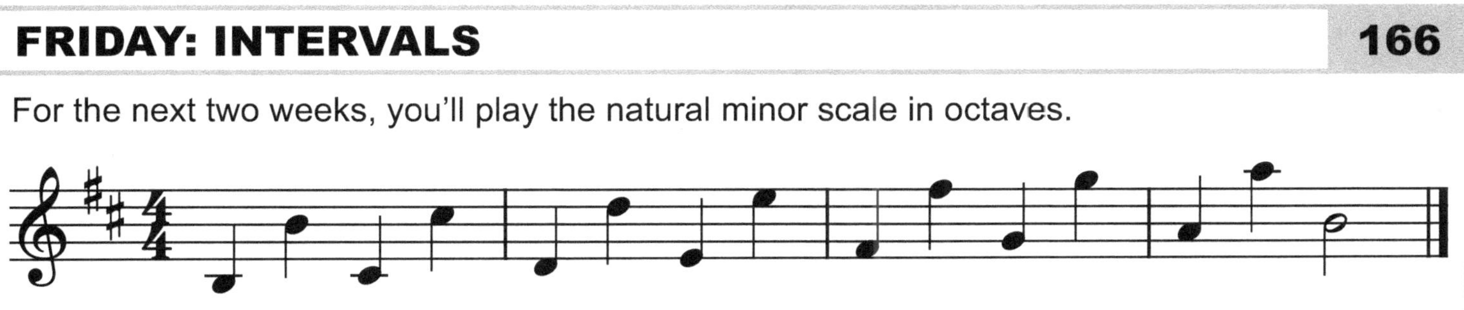

SATURDAY: ORNAMENTATION 167

Today's piece contains some accidentals. The natural sign in the second bar is a courtesy accidental to remind you to go back to the key signature after the accidental in the first bar.

SUNDAY: MUSICAL PIECE 168

Here is a nice musical piece to close out Week 24.

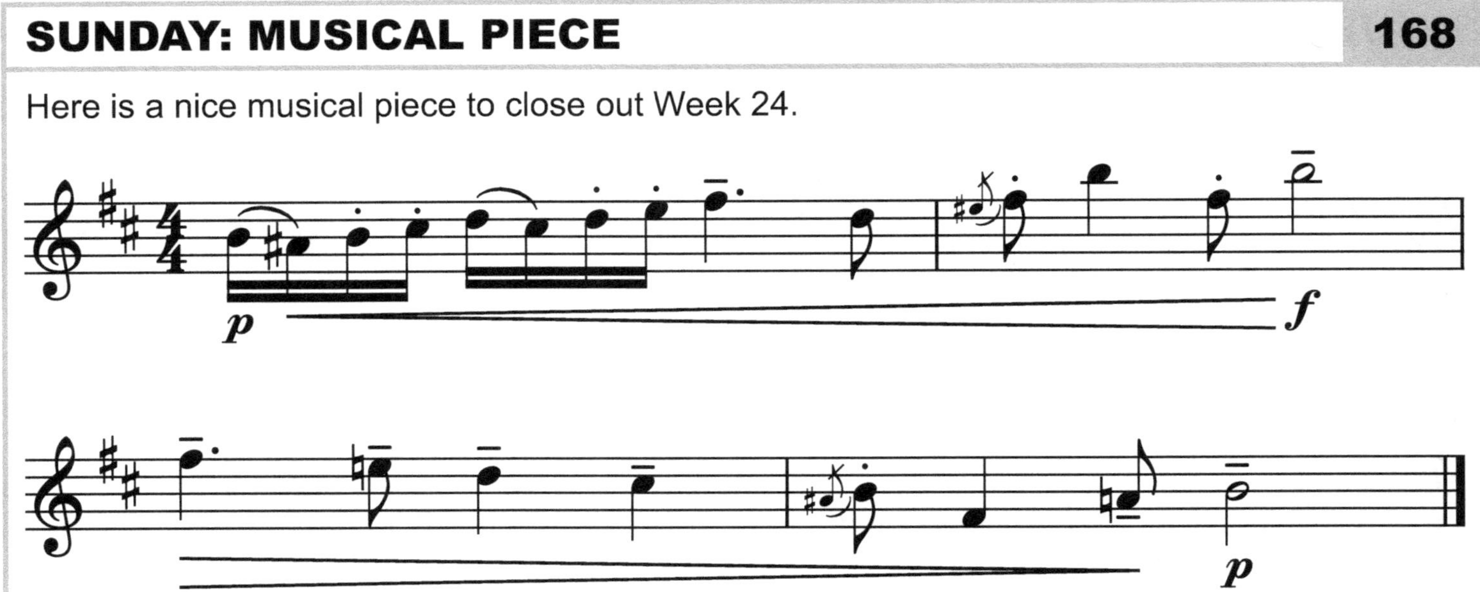

WEEK 25: F♯ NATURAL MINOR

MONDAY: LONG TONES

169

This is the last week of natural minor scales. Next week will be a review week, and then you will start working on harmonic minor scales. Here is the F♯ natural minor scale in long tones:

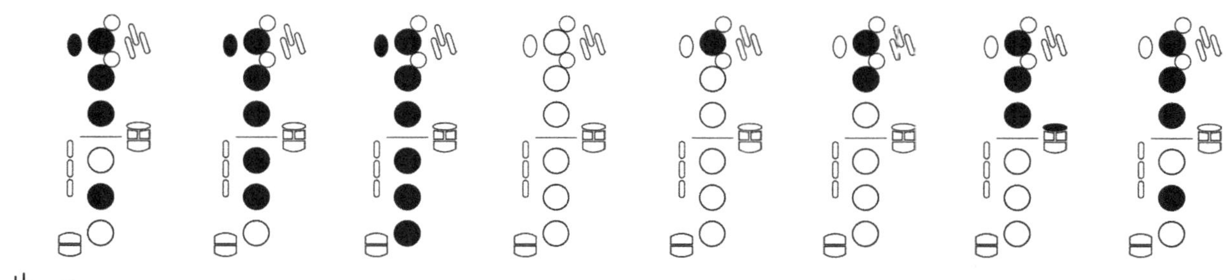

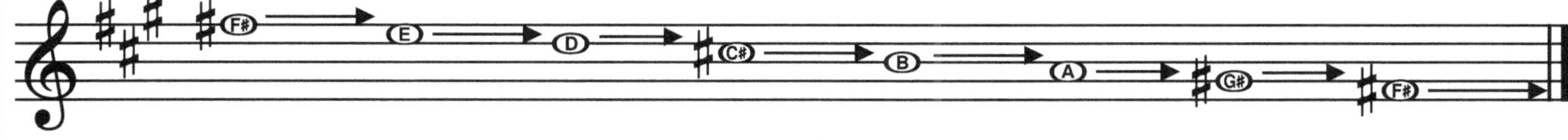

TUESDAY: RHYTHM

170

This next piece uses the dotted-8th/16th-note rhythm. You'll have to subdivide the beat into four parts to get this rhythm correct.

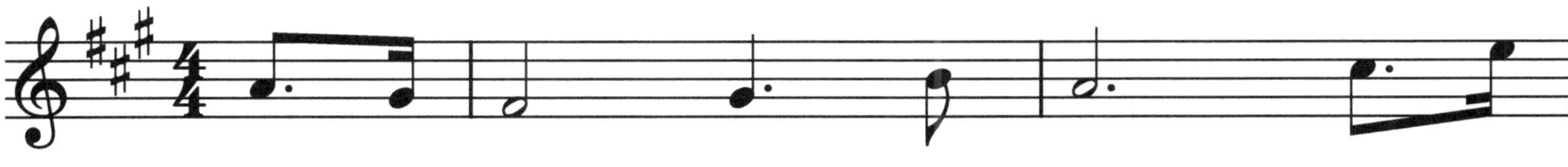

WEDNESDAY: ARTICULATION

171

Try to get the articulation and rhythms correct in this next piece. Listen to the recorded example to get an idea of how it should be played.

THURSDAY: TECHNIQUE 172

Here is your technique exercise for the week.

FRIDAY: INTERVALS 173

Don't rush this one—take your time and make sure the intonation is correct.

SATURDAY: ORNAMENTATION

174

The following piece incorporates dotted notes and a dotted-eighth-note rest.

SUNDAY: MUSICAL PIECE 175

Here is your musical piece for the week:

WEEK 26: REVIEW 2

MONDAY: LONG TONES 176

This is a review week. Today, you'll do a section of the chromatic scale in long tones.

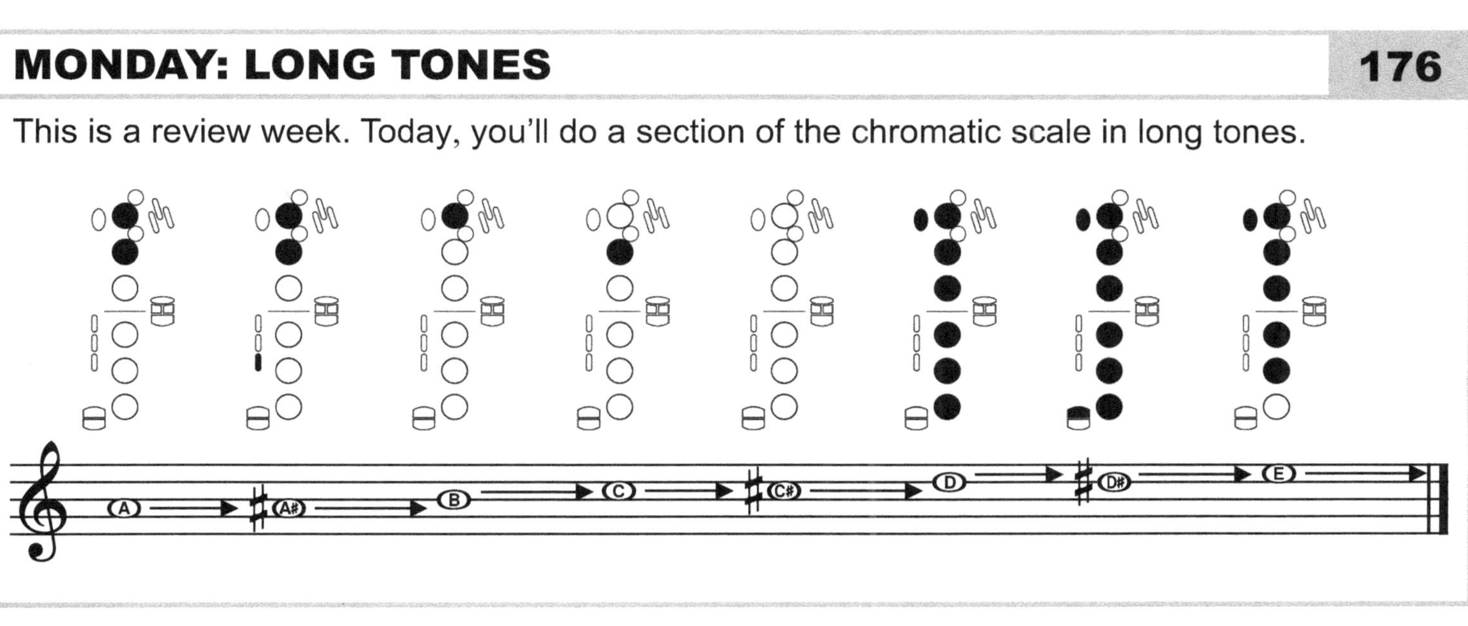

TUESDAY: RHYTHM 177

Here is a challenging little piece in the key of A (natural) minor.

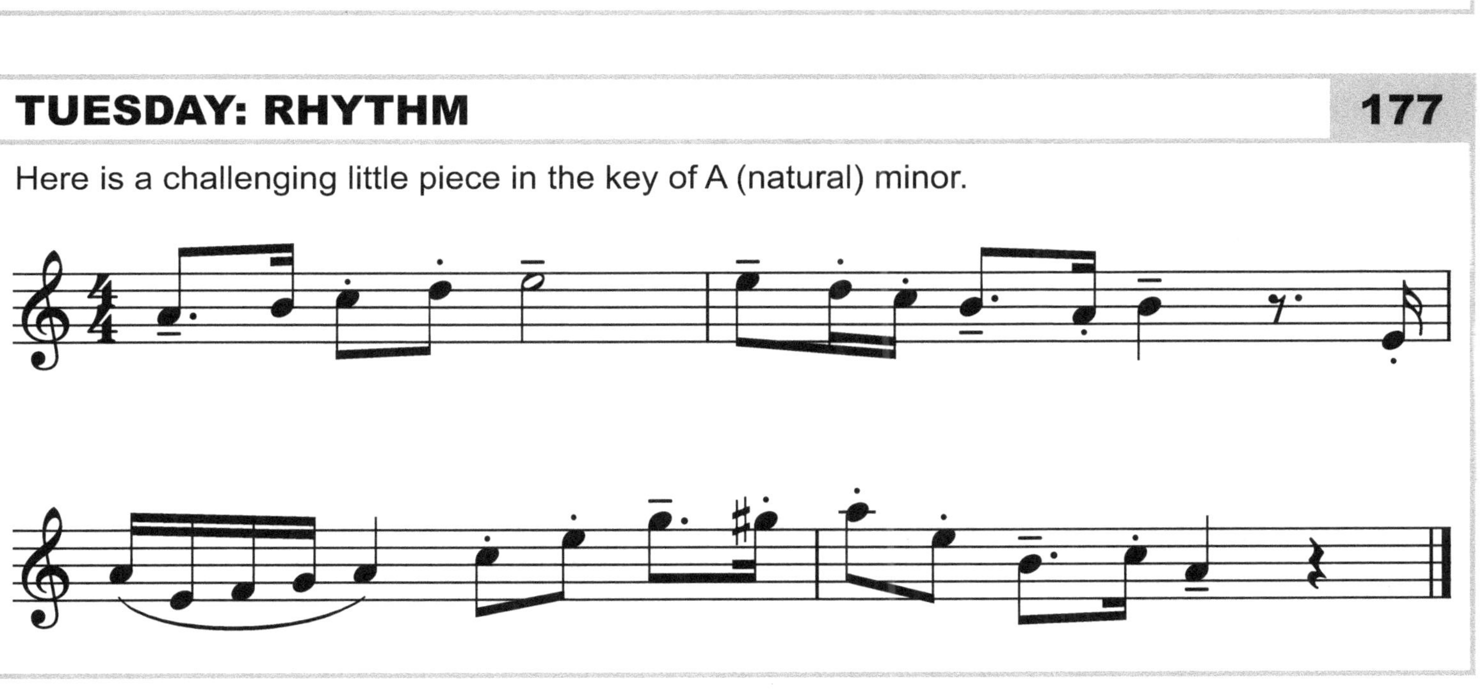

WEDNESDAY: ARTICULATION 178

Here is a nice review piece in the key of G minor.

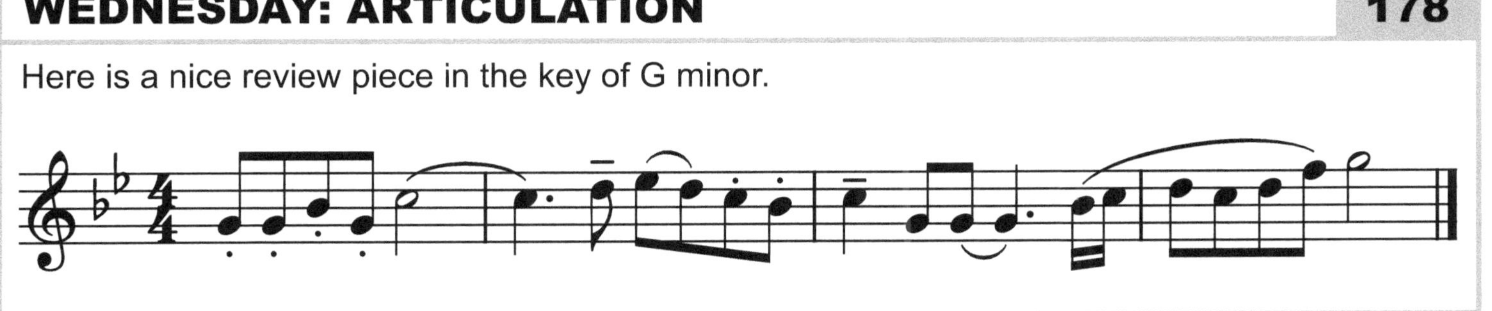

THURSDAY: TECHNIQUE 179

Your technique day review piece is in C♯ natural minor. There are a lot of 16th notes in this exercise, so start slowly and work your way up to a faster tempo.

FRIDAY: INTERVALS 180

This is the chromatic scale (all half steps). In music notation, sharps are used when ascending the scale, and flats are used when descending the scale.

SATURDAY: ORNAMENTATION 181

This review piece focuses on grace notes and a ritardando at the end.

SUNDAY: MUSICAL PIECE 182

Enjoy this last piece, in B natural minor, before starting on harmonic minor scales tomorrow.

WEEK 27: C HARMONIC MINOR

MONDAY: LONG TONES 183

Today, you'll start working on pieces that use the harmonic minor scale. This scale has a particular sound characterized by the augmented 2nd interval (three half steps) between the 6th and 7th notes.

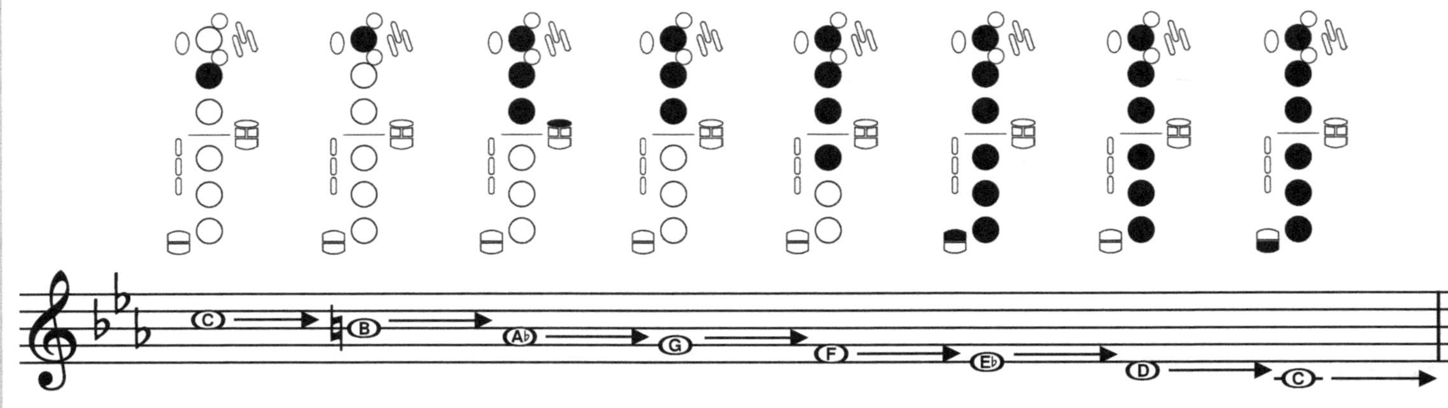

TUESDAY: RHYTHM 184

Here is this week's rhythm exercise:

WEDNESDAY: DYNAMICS & ARTICULATION 185

This piece focuses on dynamics and has a ritardando at the end.

THURSDAY: TECHNIQUE 186

Here is a nice scale technique exercise:

FRIDAY: WHOLE-TONE SCALE 187

Today, you'll play the whole-tone scale. There are two different whole-tone scales, each a half step away from each other. As the name suggests, the whole-tone scale consists entirely of whole steps.

SATURDAY: ORNAMENTATION 188

Today, you'll work on grace notes and double grace notes.

SUNDAY: MUSICAL PIECE

189

Here is your Sunday piece. Don't forget to "stop for the dot" on the trill in the last bar.

WEEK 28: F HARMONIC MINOR

MONDAY: LONG TONES **190**

Here is the F harmonic minor scale in long tones:

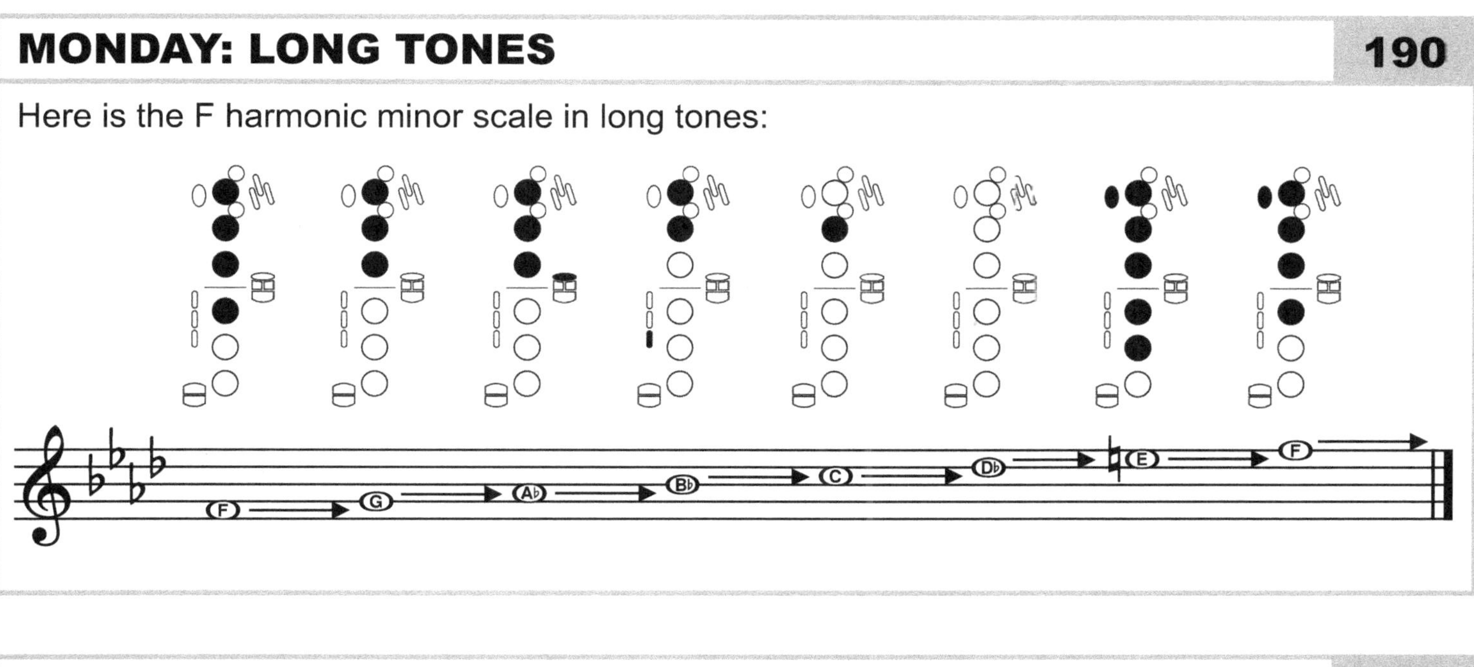

TUESDAY: RHYTHM **191**

Some of the rhythms in this next piece are difficult. Notice that the first bar starts with a 16th-note rest.

WEDNESDAY: DYNAMICS **192**

Do your best to address the dynamics and tempo change (ritardando) in this piece.

THURSDAY: TECHNIQUE **193**

Here is your technique exercise in F harmonic minor:

FRIDAY: INTERVALS **194**

This is the C whole-tone scale played in 3rds:

SATURDAY: ORNAMENTATION **195**

This exercise is a chance for you to work on your trills. Each trill should "stop for the dot"—the extra time that the dot adds.

SUNDAY: MUSICAL PIECE **196**

In the second bar of this musical piece, you'll find an exception to the "stop for the dot" rule: trill for all three beats of this dotted half note. Remember to start the trills from the above note.

WEEK 29: G HARMONIC MINOR

MONDAY: LONG TONES 197

Here is the G harmonic minor scale in long tones:

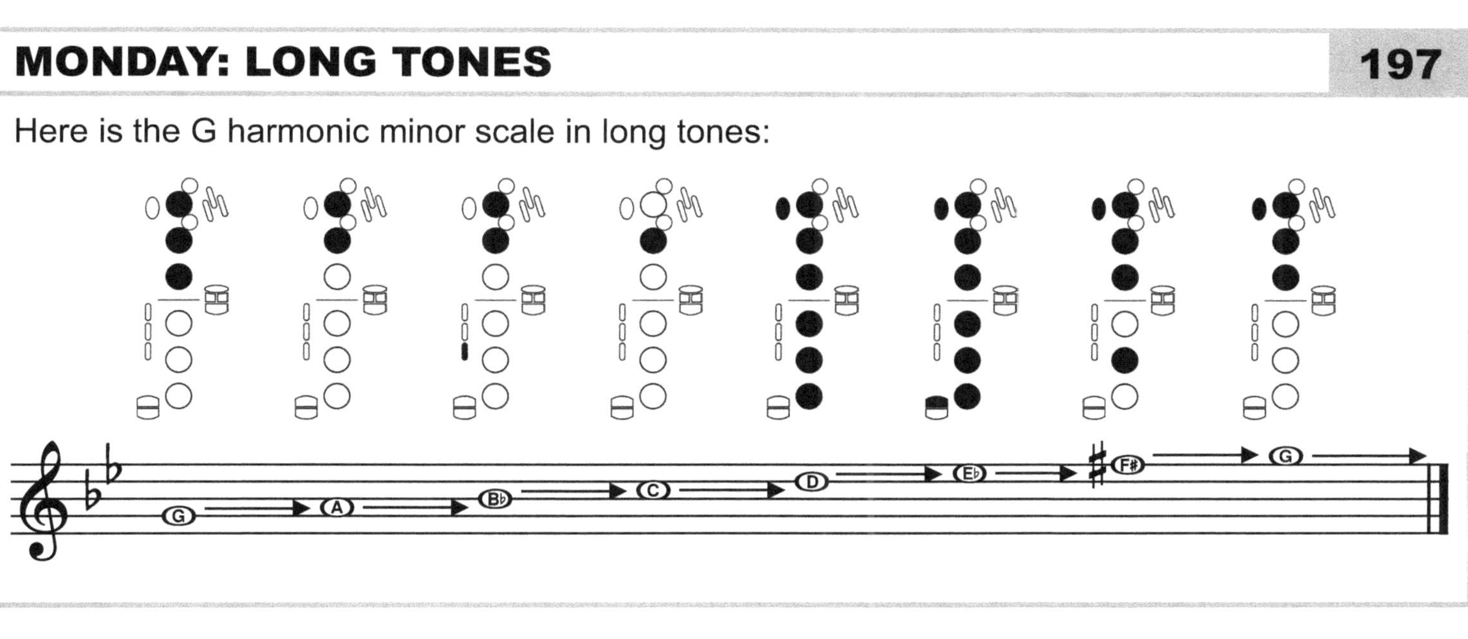

TUESDAY: RHYTHM 198

Make sure that you listen to the recorded example before starting to work on this rhythm exercise.

WEDNESDAY: DYNAMICS 199

In this piece, you'll work on dynamics and tempo changes.

THURSDAY: TECHNIQUE 200

Here is your technique piece for the week. Notice the added articulation.

FRIDAY: INTERVALS 201

Last week, you played the C whole-tone scale. This week, you'll play the D♭ whole-tone scale in 3rds.

SATURDAY: ORNAMENTATION 202

Here is an exercise for dotted-quarter-note trills. When you see an accidental above the trill marking, trill to the above note with that accidental. In other words, trill from E to F♯ in bar 3.

SUNDAY: MUSICAL PIECE

I've notated the trills in this piece with an above grace note to remind you to start the trills from the upper note.

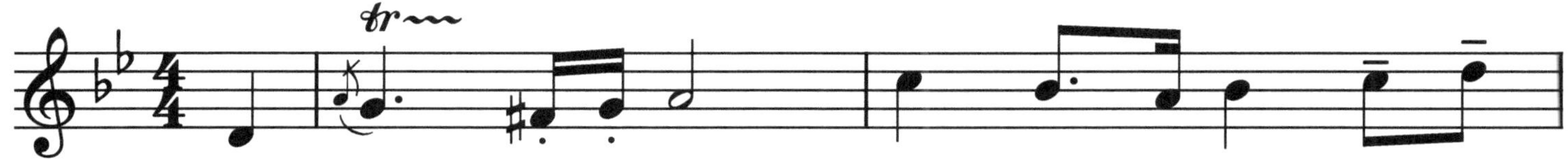

WEEK 30: B♭ HARMONIC MINOR

MONDAY: LONG TONES 204

This week, you'll work on the B♭ harmonic minor scale.

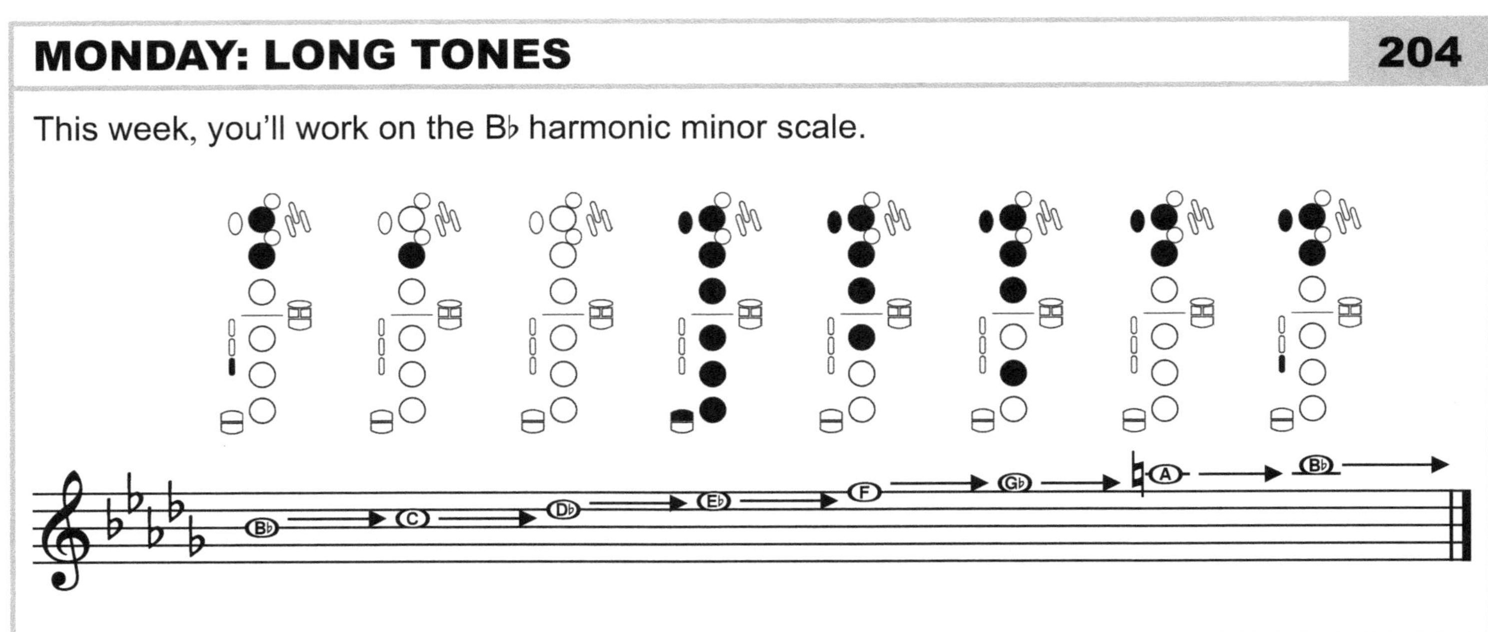

TUESDAY: RHYTHM 205

Here is your rhythm exercise for this week:

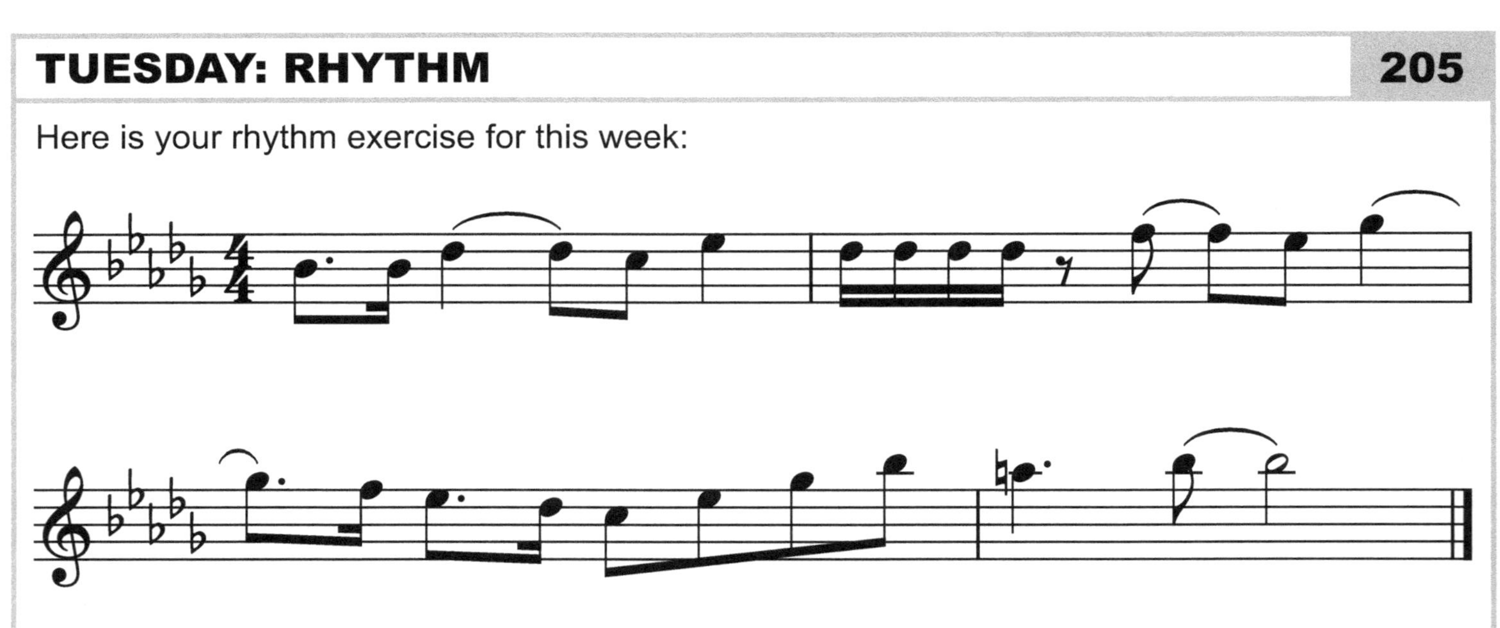

WEDNESDAY: DYNAMICS 206

This musical piece focuses on dynamics.

THURSDAY: TECHNIQUE 207

Technique and articulation are the focus of this exercise.

FRIDAY: INTERVALS 208

For interval day, you'll play all the diatonic intervals of the B♭ harmonic minor scale.

SATURDAY: ORNAMENTATION 209

In this piece, you'll work on dotted-note trills. The grace notes are added to remind you to start the trills from the above notes.

SUNDAY: MUSICAL PIECE 210

Here is a musical piece to review everything you have worked on this week.

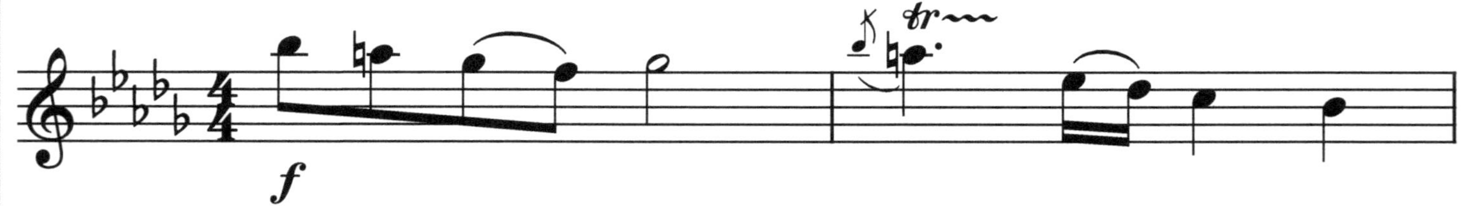

WEEK 31: D HARMONIC MINOR

MONDAY: LONG TONES 211

To start off this week, you'll play long tones while ascending the D harmonic minor scale.

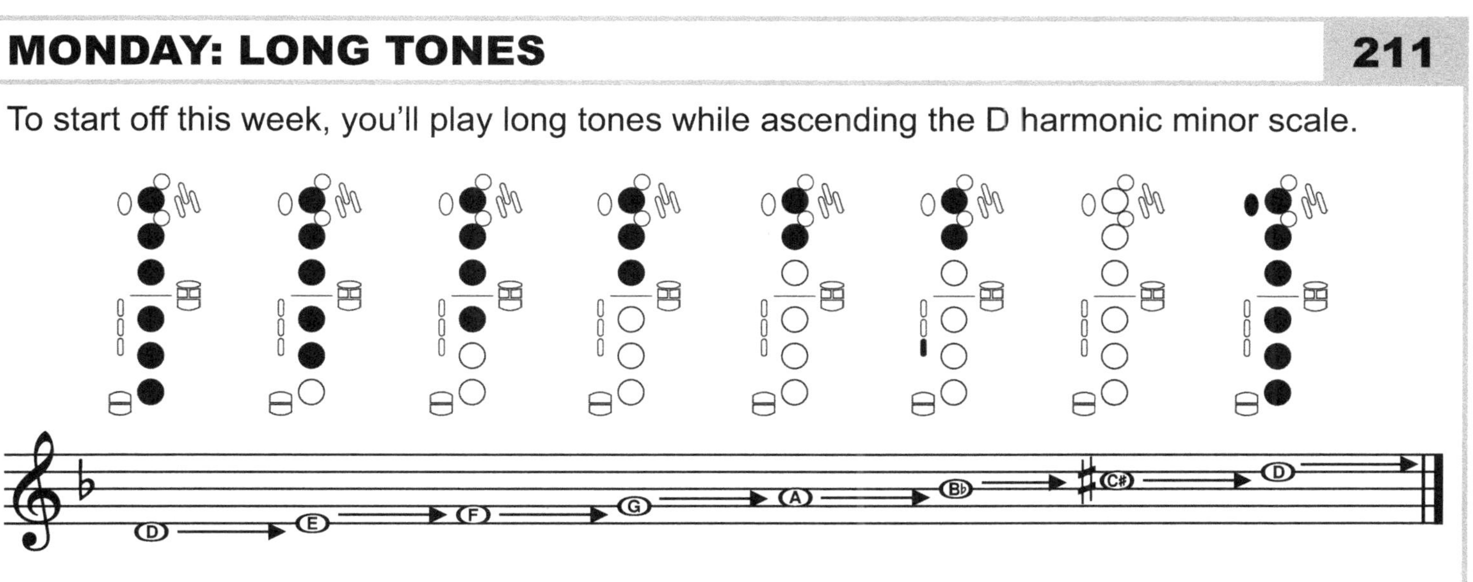

TUESDAY: RHYTHM 212

This rhythm study has some dotted-8th/16th-note rhythms in it.

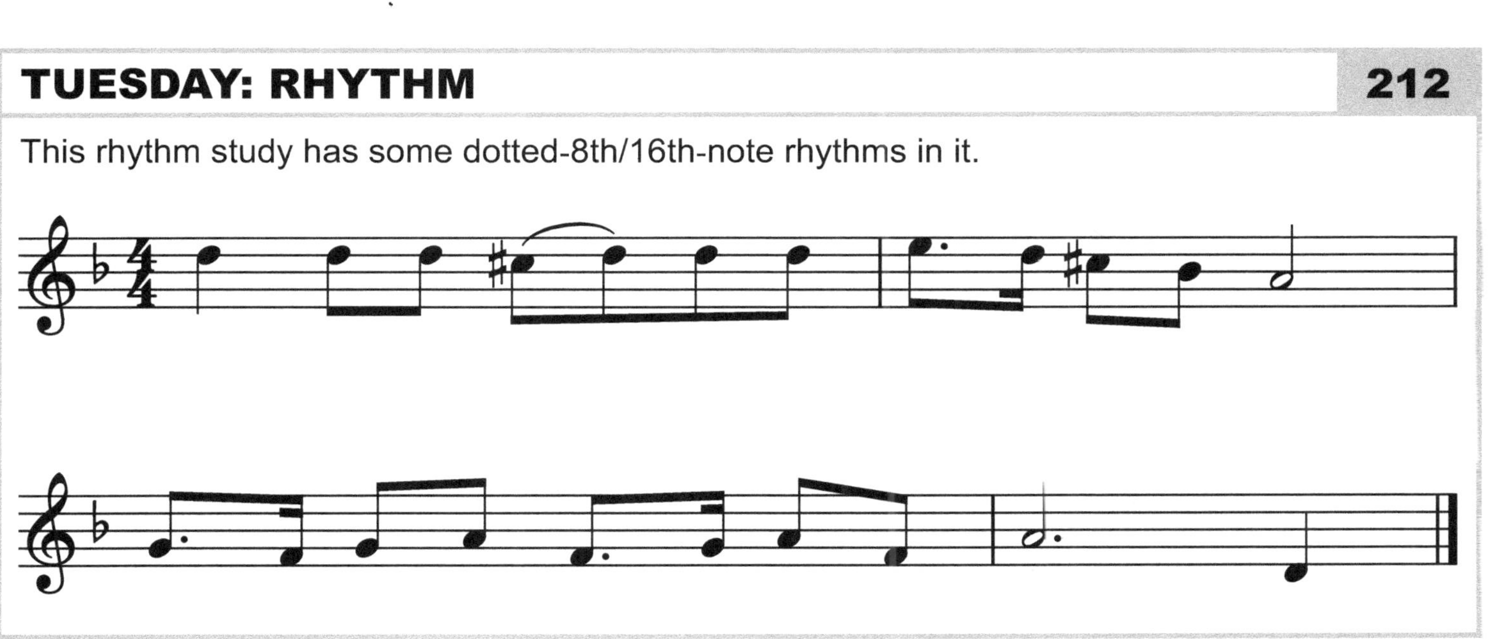

WEDNESDAY: DYNAMICS 213

Today, you'll add a crescendo to your dynamics studies. *Crescendo* means to get gradually louder and is often abbreviated as "cresc." You will also see a *fortissimo* marking, which is labeled *ff*. This is slightly louder than *forte*.

THURSDAY: TECHNIQUE 214

For this technique exercise, there will be a different articulation: tongue the first note of each grouping and slur the following three notes.

FRIDAY: INTERVALS 215

Today, you'll go through the diatonic intervals of the D harmonic minor scale. As the intervals get wider, keep your embouchure flexible and try to hear the intonation of the notes before you play them.

SATURDAY: ARTICULATION 216

You'll see a new articulation in this piece, an *accent*, which is a ">" marking above or below the notehead that indicates the note should receive extra emphasis, either through stronger articulation, increased volume, or both. Listen to the recorded example to get an idea of how to play these accents.

SUNDAY: MUSICAL PIECE 217

Here is a musical piece containing the material that you accomplished this week. The *fortissimo* marking underneath the first note is unnecessary because of the accent mark, but it was included to remind you to play this note louder.

WEEK 32: E♭ HARMONIC MINOR

MONDAY: LONG TONES 218

Here are your long tones for the week. This is the E♭ harmonic minor scale.

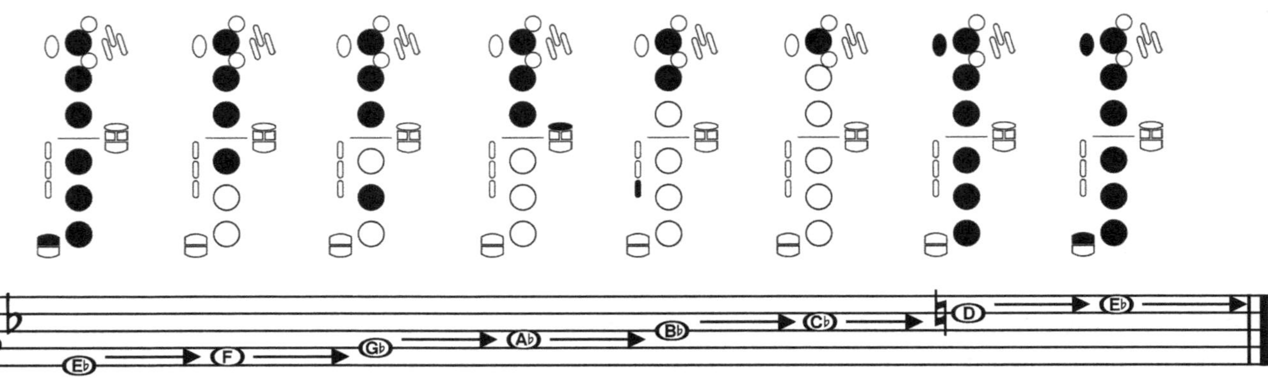

TUESDAY: RHYTHM 219

This exercise contains some very difficult rhythms. I suggest that you work on it one bar at a time and then put it all together.

WEDNESDAY: DYNAMICS 220

This piece has a *diminuendo* that goes all the way down to a new dynamic, *pianissimo*, which is softer than *piano*.

THURSDAY: TECHNIQUE **221**

Here is a technique exercise with an articulation of slur 3/tongue 1:

FRIDAY: INTERVALS **222**

Your interval practice this week will consist of the diatonic intervals of the E♭ harmonic minor scale.

SATURDAY: ARTICULATION **223**

Today is a review of articulation that you've worked on so far. Notice that some notes have two articulations. You will add an extra attack at the beginning of the note for the accent and then hold the note for its entire duration for the tenuto marking.

SUNDAY: MUSICAL PIECE

224

Here is your musical piece for the week. In the first full bar, you'll see a slur going to a staccato note. This means that you cut the staccato note short without tonguing it. Listen to the recorded example to hear the articulation.

WEEK 33: A HARMONIC MINOR

MONDAY: LONG TONES 225

There will be a few new things this week. Enjoy the musical pieces in A harmonic minor. But first, here are your long tones.

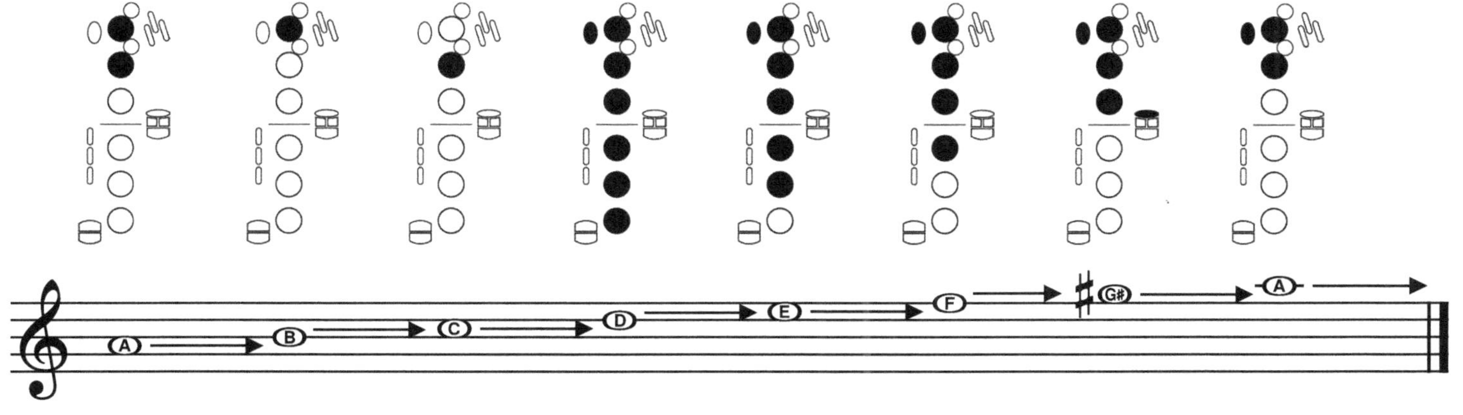

TUESDAY: RHYTHM 226

Today, you'll add triplets to your rhythm studies. This is a group of three notes played over the same amount of time as two notes of equivalent value. You want to evenly space the three notes over the allotted time. Listen to the recorded example before trying this piece. (**Tip:** Say "tri-pu-let" to get an idea of how to evenly space the notes.)

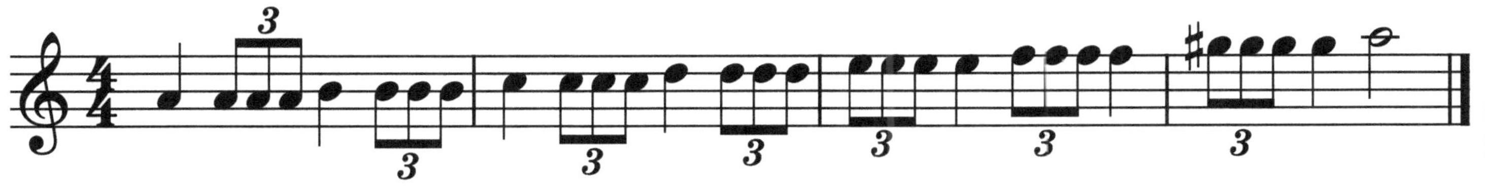

WEDNESDAY: DYNAMICS 227

The following piece contains some interesting dynamic contrast.

THURSDAY: TECHNIQUE 228

Here, the A harmonic minor scale is played in a slur 2/tongue 2 style of articulation.

FRIDAY: INTERVALS 229

Today, you'll play all the diatonic intervals of the A harmonic minor scale, moving high to low.

SATURDAY: ARTICULATION 230

The squiggly lines above the notes in the second and fourth bars are called *mordents*, which are like trills (you can use trill fingerings) except you only go up to the adjacent note one time and then come back down. It's important that you place the emphasis on the beginning of the note. Mordents are usually played in a quick fashion, but how fast you play them depends on the context of the piece of music. Listen to the recorded example to get an idea before starting this exercise.

SUNDAY: MUSICAL PIECE 231

Here is your musical piece for the week. Enjoy!

WEEK 34: A♭ HARMONIC MINOR

MONDAY: LONG TONES 232

This week's focus is on the A♭ harmonic minor scale. Be careful: C♭ and F♭ are the same as B-natural and E-natural, respectively.

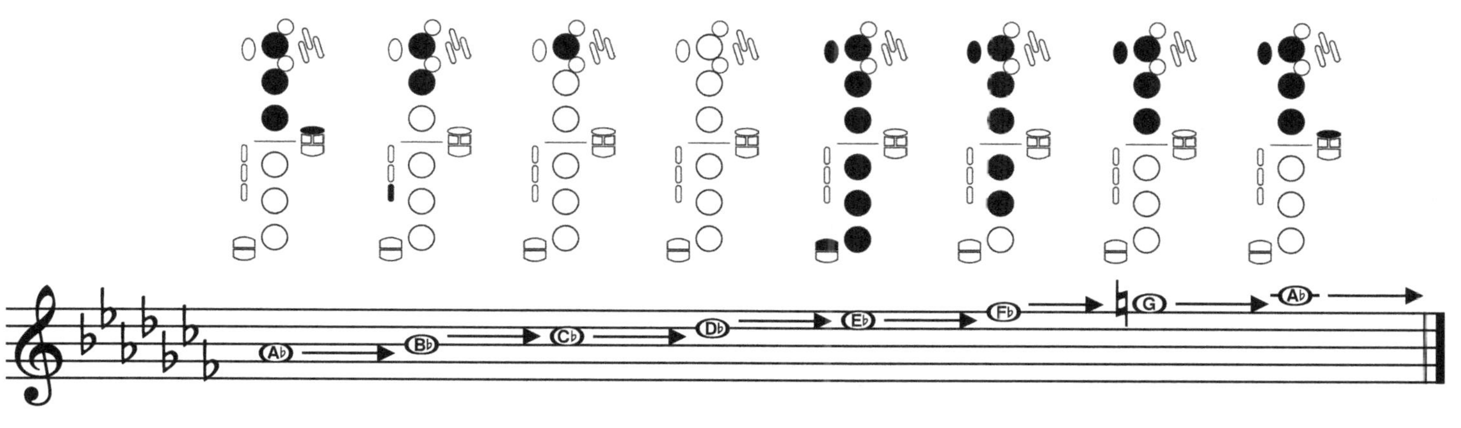

TUESDAY: RHYTHM 233

Here is a fun rhythmic piece with some triplets.

WEDNESDAY: DYNAMICS 234

In this next piece, start the trill from the above note. Remember that you are trilling to F♭ (E-natural). There is a "fake" fingering (D♯ to E) for this trill in the trill chart at the beginning of the book.

THURSDAY: TECHNIQUE 235

This is a challenging technique exercise, as it requires you to play the scale in groups of 4 with specific articulation.

FRIDAY: INTERVALS 236

Here are the diatonic intervals of the A♭ harmonic minor scale, played from the high root down.

SATURDAY: ARTICULATION 237

In this piece, you'll be working on mordents and dotted notes with trills. There is also a ritardando at the end of the piece.

SUNDAY: MUSICAL PIECE

238

Have fun working on this piece. But first, take some time to inspect all of its embellishments and dynamics.

WEEK 35: E HARMONIC MINOR

MONDAY: LONG TONES 239

Here are your long tones for the week, played with the E harmonic minor scale:

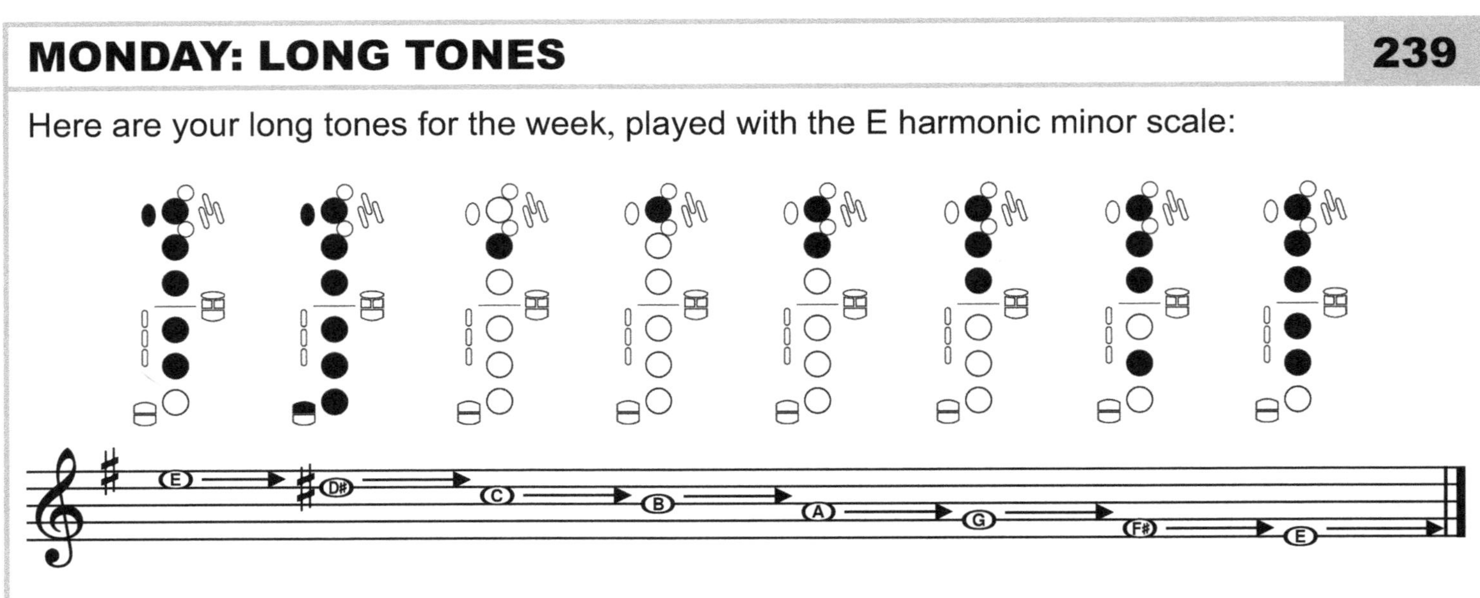

TUESDAY: RHYTHM 240

Here is your rhythm piece for the week. There should be a distinct difference between the triplets and the dotted-8th/16th rhythm in the third measure.

WEDNESDAY: DYNAMICS

241

The following piece has a crescendo at the beginning and a diminuendo at the end.

THURSDAY: TECHNIQUE

242

Here is the E harmonic minor scale in groups of 4, played with a slur 3/tongue 1 articulation:

FRIDAY: INTERVALS

243

Here are the diatonic intervals of the E harmonic minor scale:

SATURDAY: ARTICULATION 244

This nice piece of music incorporates some mordents and a trill.

SUNDAY: MUSICAL PIECE 245

Welcome to your musical wrap-up piece for the week. I hope you're enjoying the book so far!

WEEK 36: C♯ HARMONIC MINOR

MONDAY: LONG TONES 246

Here is the C♯ harmonic minor scale in long tones:

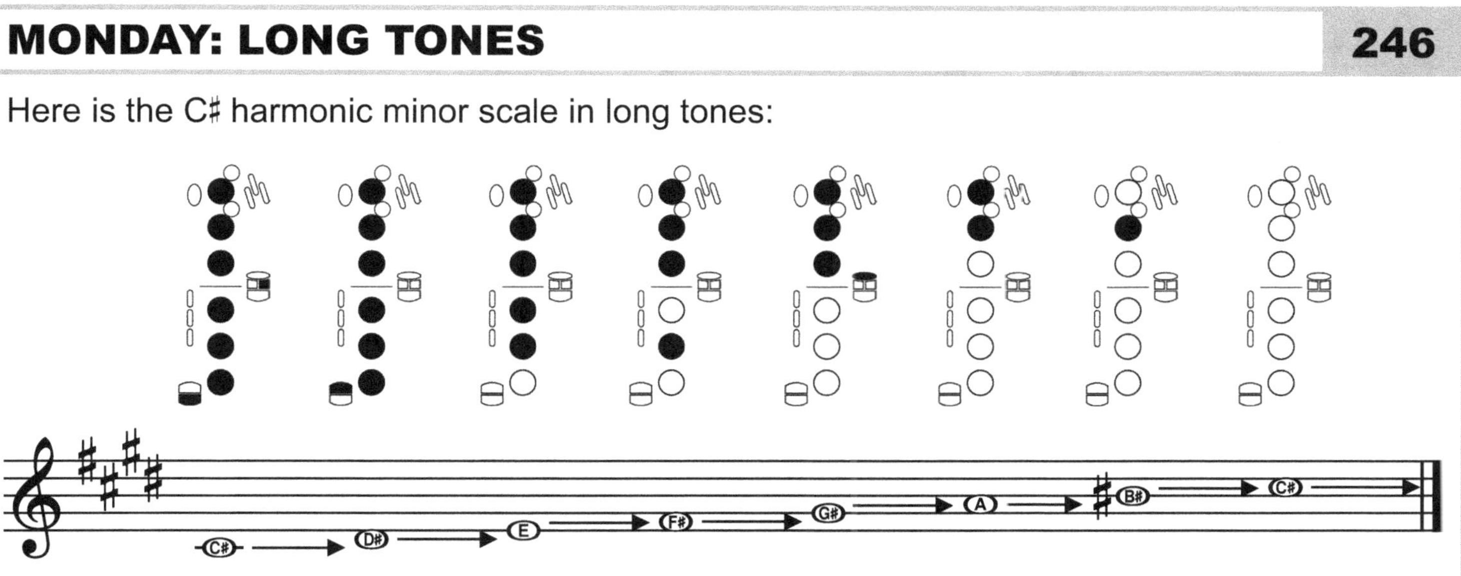

TUESDAY: RHYTHM 247

Today, you'll play all of the diatonic 7th chords of the C♯ harmonic minor scale with a triplet rhythm.

WEDNESDAY: DYNAMICS 248

This piece has some dynamic changes and a couple of mordents.

THURSDAY: TECHNIQUE 249

Here is your technique exercise for the week:

FRIDAY: INTERVALS 250

Here are all the diatonic intervals of the C♯ harmonic minor scale, played with slurs. As the intervals get wider, the slurs will get more difficult.

SATURDAY: ARTICULATION 251

The time signature of this piece is 3/4—three quarter notes per measure. In this time signature, you'll place extra emphasis on the first note of each measure. I've placed an accent on the first note of each measure as a reminder; however, you will not see this normally written in the music. Listen to the recorded example to get an idea.

SUNDAY: MUSICAL PIECE 252

Here is your musical piece for the week, written in 3/4 time:

WEEK 37: B HARMONIC MINOR

MONDAY: LONG TONES 253

The scale for this week is B harmonic minor.

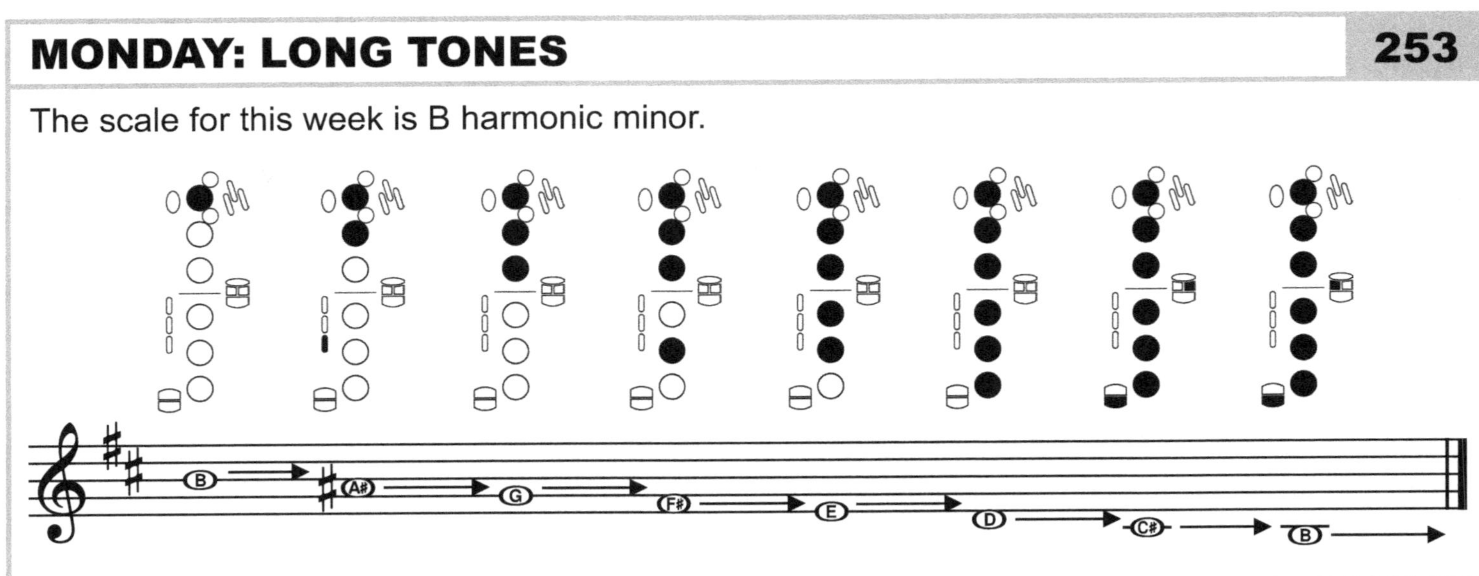

TUESDAY: RHYTHM 254

Here are the diatonic triads of the B harmonic minor scale in triplets.

WEDNESDAY: DYNAMICS 255

This piece contains a *fermata*, which means the note is to be held longer than its usual allotted time. The length of the note is up to the player.

THURSDAY: TECHNIQUE 256

Today, you'll play the B harmonic minor scale. In this exercise, you'll slur in groups of 4, tonguing only the first note of each note grouping.

FRIDAY: INTERVALS 257

Here are the diatonic intervals of the B harmonic minor scale descending with slurs:

SATURDAY: ARTICULATION 258

This piece is in 3/4 time. You'll see a new articulation called *marcato*, which is like an accent except usually a little stronger and shorter. Notice that, even though it is short, the second note is tied to the third note. I have written it like this because it's easier to read than an eighth note and an eighth-note rest.

SUNDAY: MUSICAL PIECE 259

To end the week, here is a simple little piece with a trill and a ritardando at the end:

WEEK 38: F♯ HARMONIC MINOR

MONDAY: LONG TONES 260

You made it to Week 38! Today, you'll be using the F♯ harmonic minor scale.

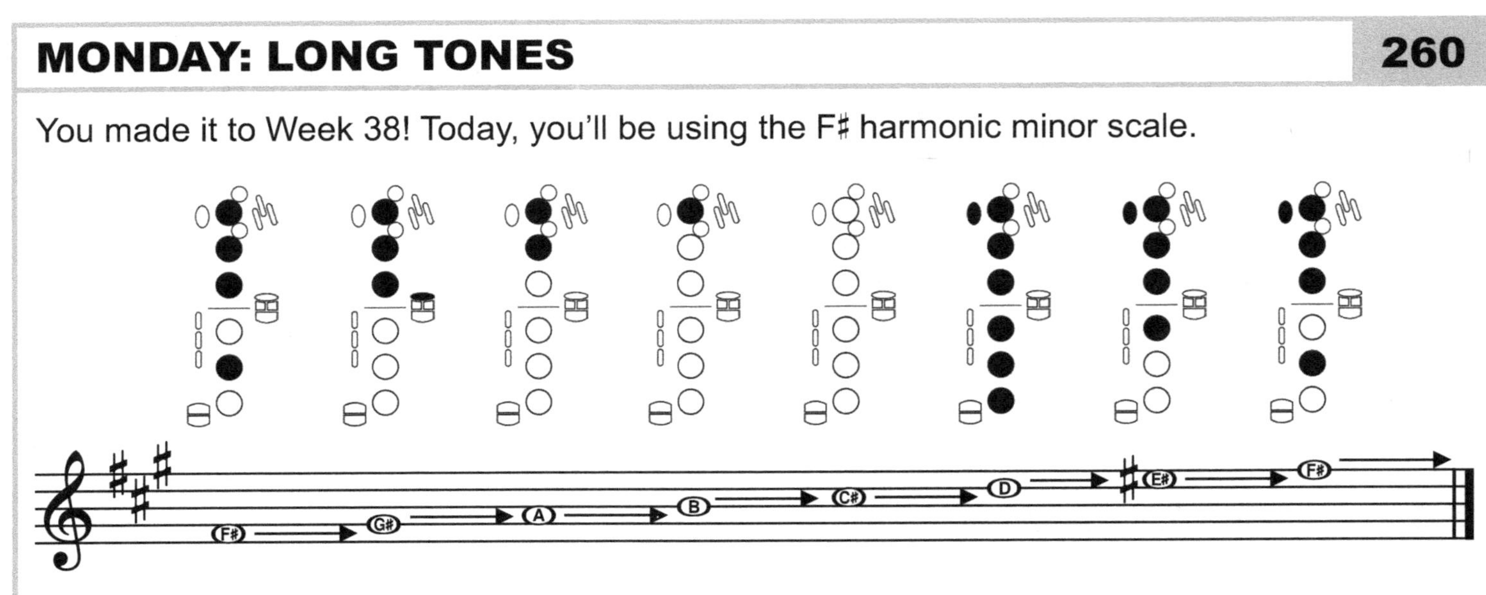

TUESDAY: RHYTHM 261

Today, you'll play the F♯ harmonic minor scale in triads, using a triplet rhythm.

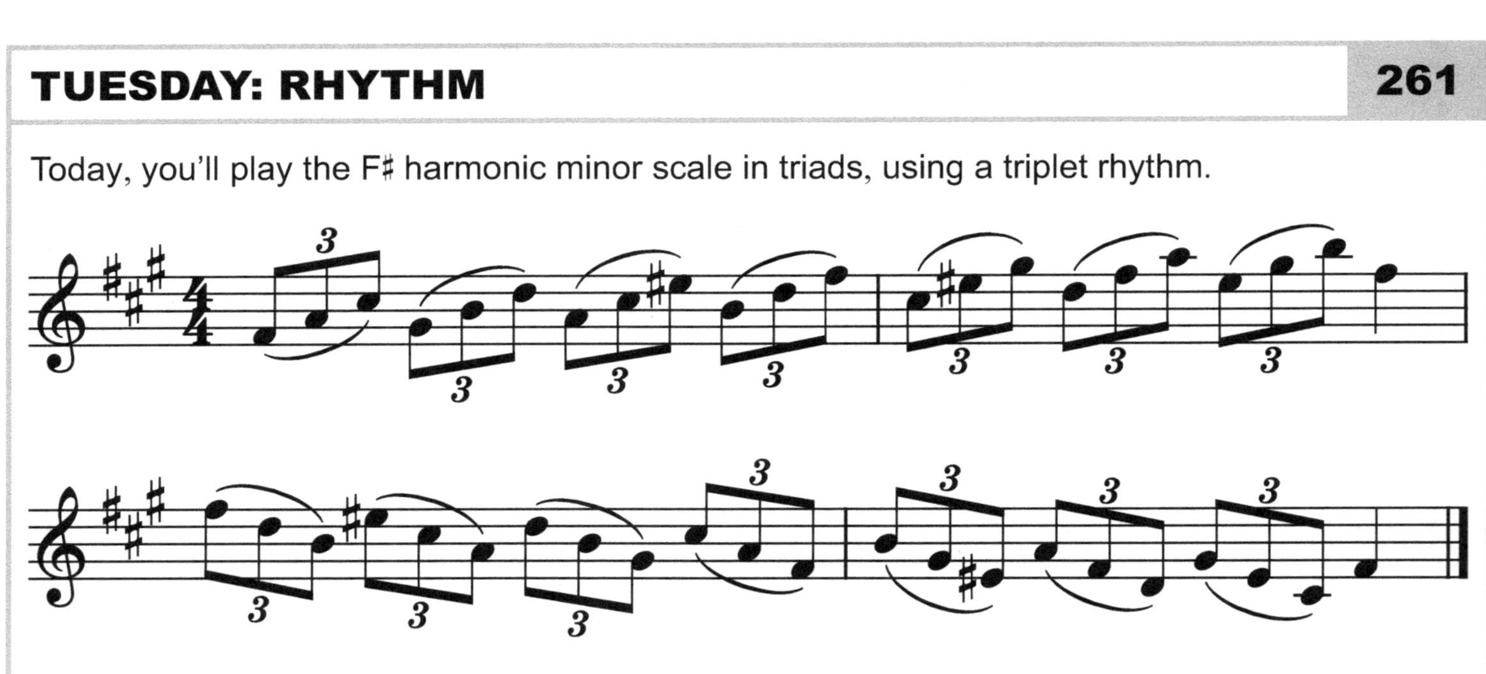

WEDNESDAY: DYNAMICS

262

This is a nice little piece to work on dynamics.

THURSDAY: TECHNIQUE

263

This next piece is a good workout for your tongue. If your tongue is having a hard time keeping up with the tempo, emphasizing the first note of each grouping a little bit should help.

FRIDAY: INTERVALS

264

In this piece, you'll play all of the diatonic intervals of the F♯ harmonic minor scale with a triplet rhythm.

SATURDAY: ARTICULATION 265

Here is a piece that focuses on articulation, particularly marcato notes.

SUNDAY: MUSICAL PIECE 266

In today's musical piece, the accented notes should be held slightly longer than the marcato note.

WEEK 39: REVIEW 3

MONDAY: LONG TONES 267

This week will be a review of what you have worked on for the past 12 weeks. Next week, you'll start working on the blues scale. Today, you'll play long tones over a section of the chromatic scale.

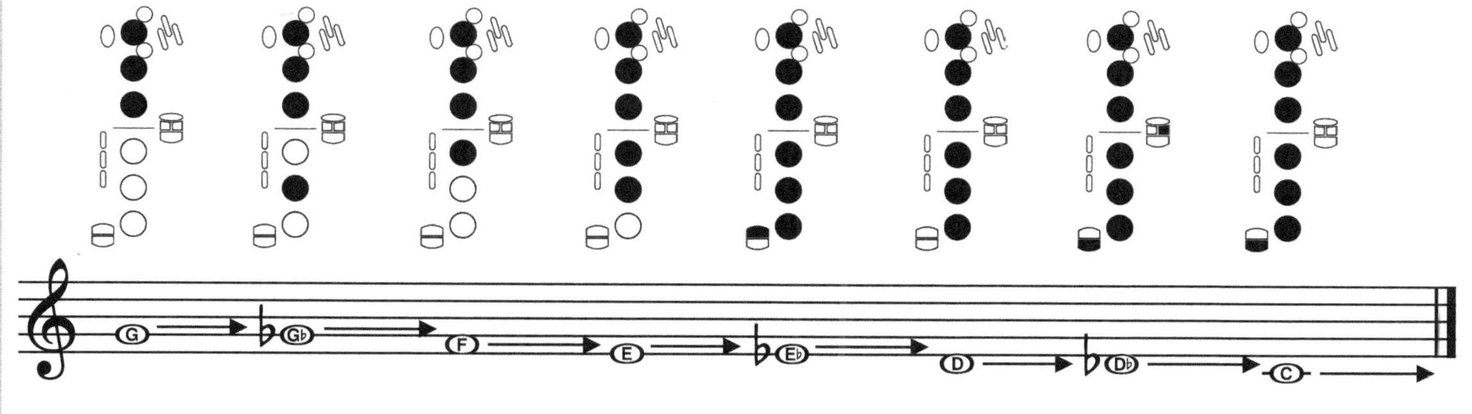

TUESDAY: RHYTHM 268

In today's piece, you'll go through all the rhythms that you have worked on so far.

WEDNESDAY: DYNAMICS 269

This review piece focuses on dynamics and the B harmonic minor scale.

THURSDAY: TECHNIQUE 270

This is a difficult technique piece using the chromatic scale. Make sure that your 16th notes are as even as possible. Keep your fingers close to the keys when not depressed to maximize your efficiency.

FRIDAY: INTERVALS 271

Here are all the intervals of one octave of the chromatic scale:

SATURDAY: ARTICULATION 272

This piece is in 3/4 time, with a long ritardando at the end. The fermata on the last note means to hold it longer than usual.

SUNDAY: SWING EIGHTH NOTES **273**

Until now, you have been playing "straight" eighth notes in a classical style. Starting today, and for the majority of the rest of this book, you will be playing *swing eighth notes*, or uneven eighth notes. The notes on the downbeats (1, 2, 3, and 4) are approximately twice as long as the notes on the upbeats. In addition to this "unevenness," the upbeat is often articulated and given more emphasis. I will be adding some typical swing articulation for the next couple weeks to help you get used to swing eighth notes.

Today's musical piece is in 3/4 time and the eighth notes will be played in a swing style. Usually, articulation in swing music is just understood after years of experience. However, I have added articulation to help you get going for the next few weeks. I have also added accents to remind you to add extra emphasis to the upbeats. Listen to the recorded example to get a feel for this musical piece.

WEEK 40: C BLUES SCALE

MONDAY: LONG TONES 274

For the next six weeks, you'll be working with the blues scale. The *blues scale* is essential to jazz, blues, rock, and all contemporary music. You'll notice a "bluesy" sound within the scale, especially around the flatted 3rd, 5th, and 7th degrees. Here is the C blues scale in long tones:

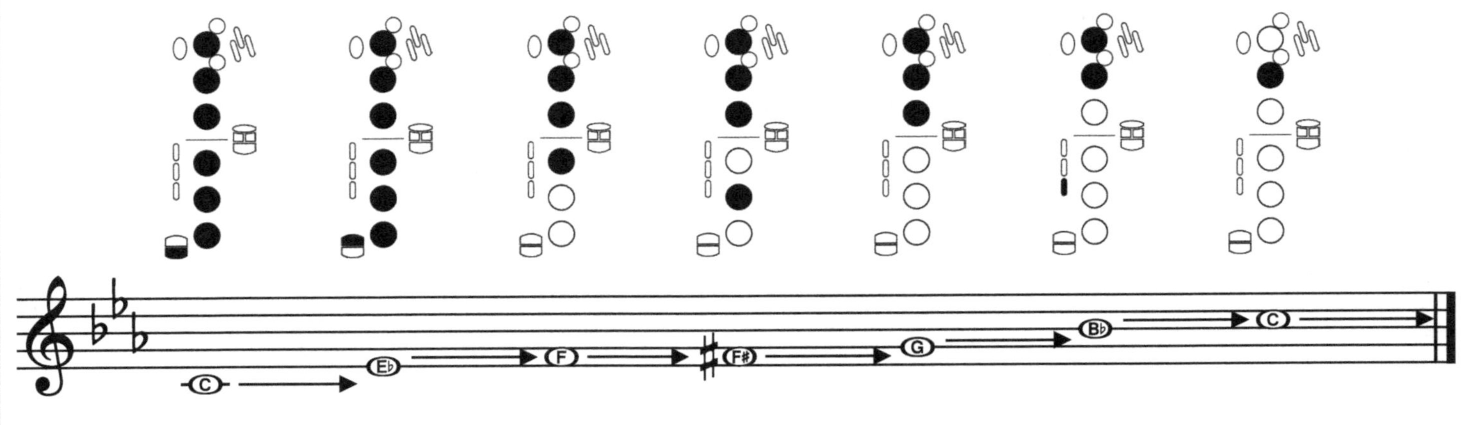

TUESDAY: ARTICULATION 275

Let's work on your swing-eighth-note articulation! Listen to the recording and work your way up in tempo.

WEDNESDAY: THE BLUE NOTE 276

In the C blues scale, F♯ is called the "blue note." This note has a very dissonant quality when played alone; however, when played in conjunction with neighboring notes, it can create a great bluesy quality.

THURSDAY: ARTICULATION 277

Here is another piece in a swing style to work on!

FRIDAY: RHYTHM 278

Listen to the recording of this one to get the rhythms and the inflections with the grace notes.

SATURDAY: ARTICULATION 279

By now, you've probably noticed that, in general, with swing eighth notes, you tongue the notes on the upbeats and slur into the notes on the downbeats. There are always exceptions, depending on the context of the music. I will notate some of these and then, after a while, you'll be able to do this naturally.

SUNDAY: MUSICAL PIECE 280

This piece is in a ballad style. As you listen to the accompanying recording, notice how the feel of swing eighth notes changes when the tempo changes.

WEEK 41: F & G BLUES SCALES

MONDAY: LONG TONES 281

For the rest of this book, you'll be covering two keys per week. Mondays and Thursdays will be long-tone days, and the rest of the days will be musical pieces. Here is the F blues scale in long tones:

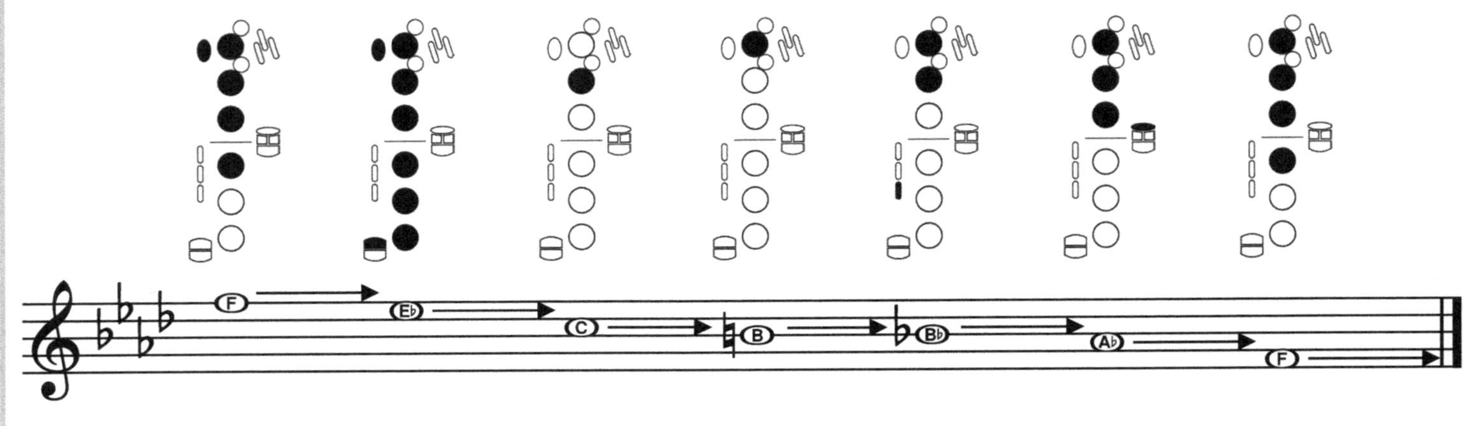

TUESDAY: RHYTHM 282

In this musical piece, you'll notice that each phrase starts the same way but has a different ending. This is a common technique in composition and improvisation. The first phrase is considered a "question," while the second phrase is the "answer."

WEDNESDAY: ARTICULATION 283

This piece really gives you a chance to work on your swing eighth notes. Listen to the recorded example and follow the written articulation.

THURSDAY: LONG TONES 284

Here is the G blues scale in long tones:

G B♭ C C♯ D F G

FRIDAY: RHYTHM 285

Here is a swing piece in 3/4 time:

SATURDAY: ARTICULATION 286

As you work on these swing pieces, you'll start to notice that certain notes require more emphasis, depending on their context. This emphasis is not always written into the music. Listen to the recorded example to hear which notes are accented more, and which are accented less.

SUNDAY: MUSICAL PIECE 287

In the beginning of this piece, the notes on the offbeats are played with a short articulation and a bit of an accent. As written, they're tied to the subsequent notes simply to make it easier to read.

WEEK 42: B♭ & D BLUES SCALES

MONDAY: LONG TONES 288

Here is the B♭ blues scale in long tones:

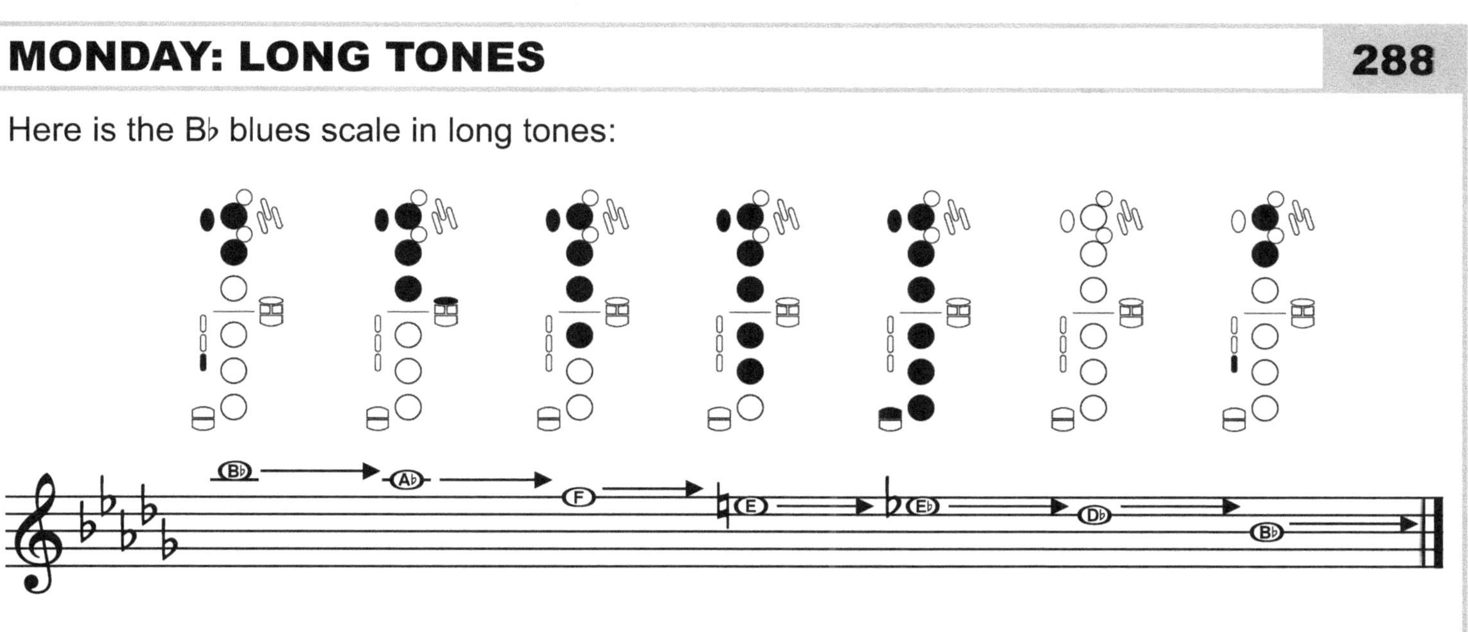

TUESDAY: RHYTHM 289

Notice how this piece has one two-bar “question” phrase and one two-bar “answer” phrase.

WEDNESDAY: ARTICULATION 290

Some of these rhythms are played differently in a swing style than when you play them in a classical piece. Listen to the recorded example to get the proper feel for the triplet in bar 3.

THURSDAY: LONG TONES 291

Here is the D blues scale:

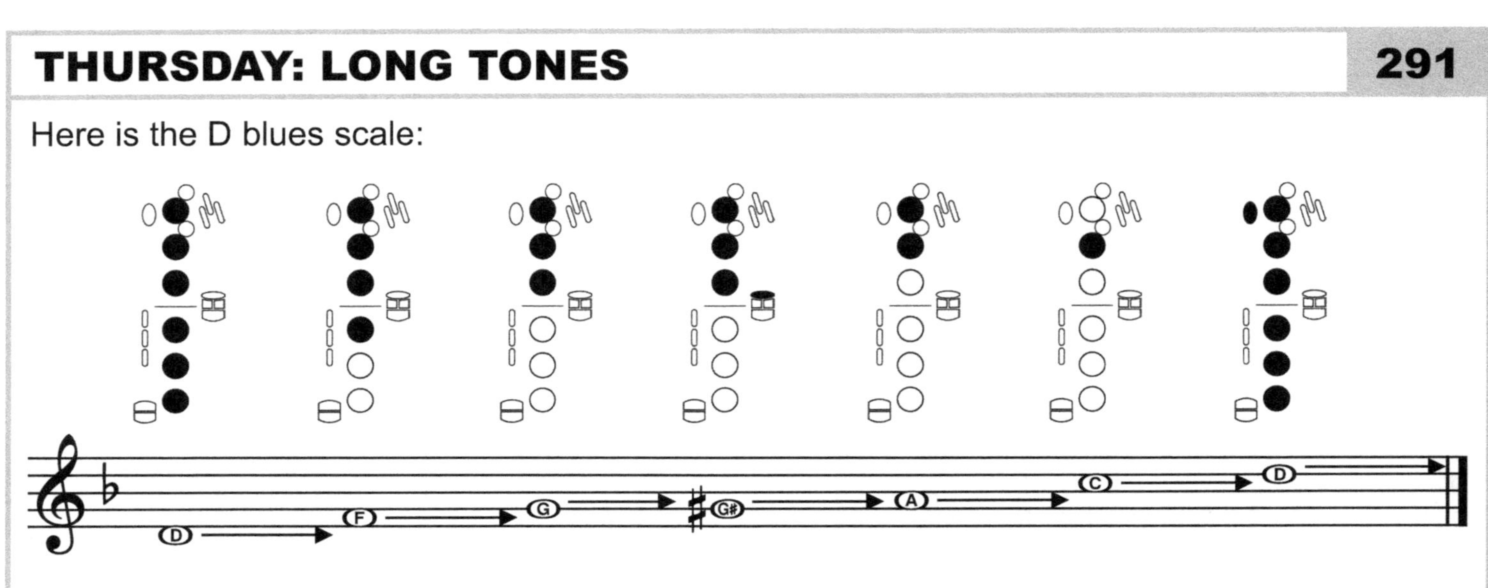

FRIDAY: RHYTHM 292

Here is another slower piece:

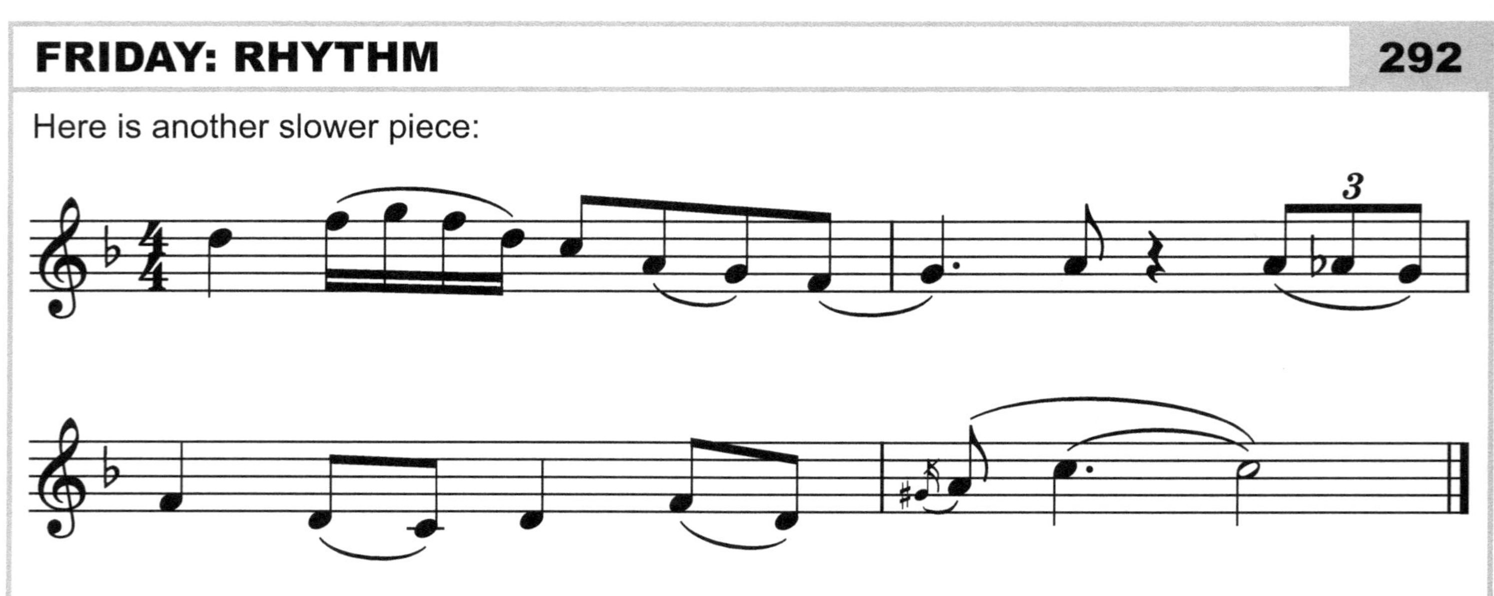

SATURDAY: ARTICULATION

293

This piece is played in a ballad style.

SUNDAY: MUSICAL PIECE

294

To finish off your week, here is a nice, bright, tempo swing piece for you:

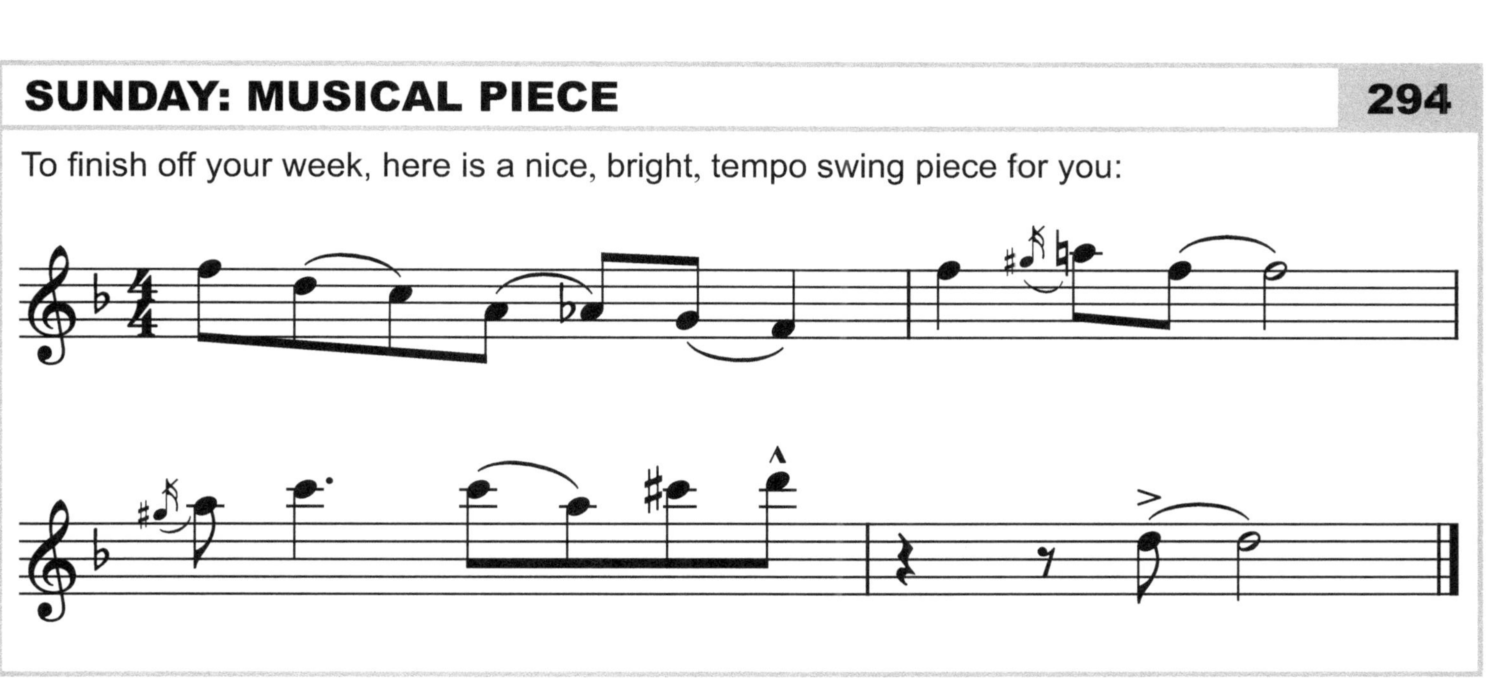

WEEK 43: E♭ & A BLUES SCALES

MONDAY: LONG TONES 295

Here is the E♭ blues scale in long tones:

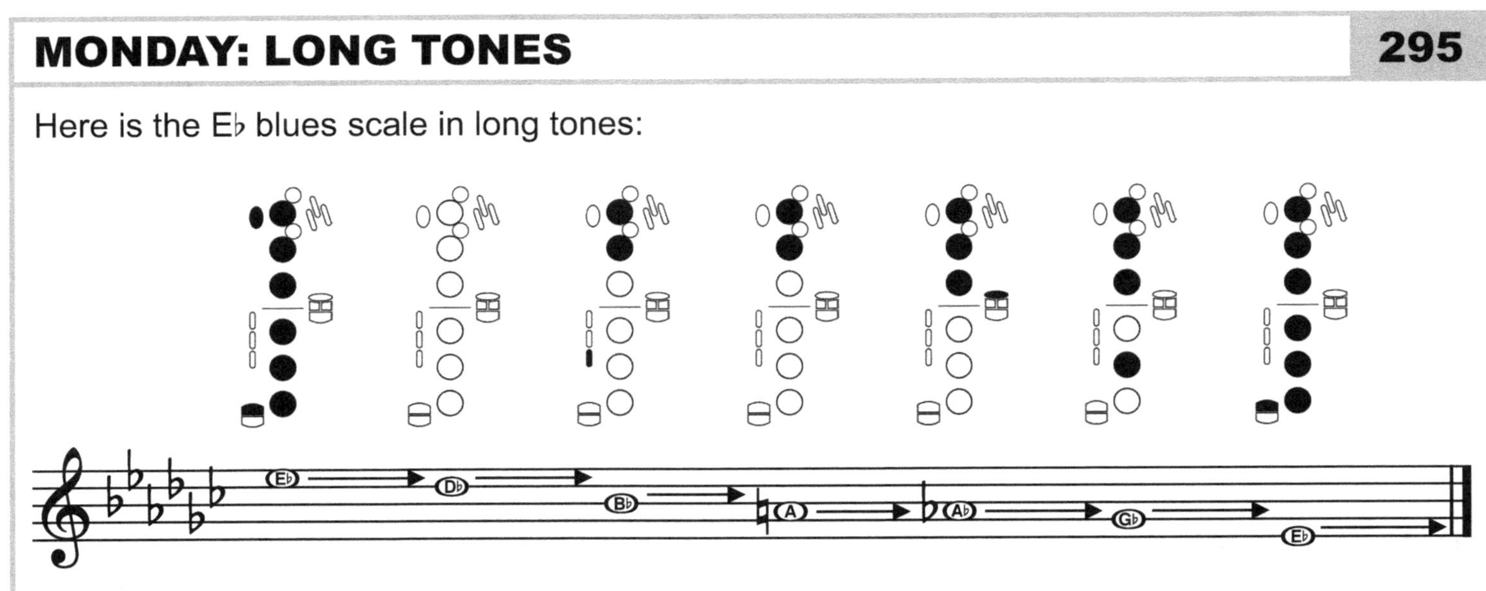

TUESDAY: RHYTHM 296

This piece has the feel of a shuffle.

WEDNESDAY: ARTICULATION 297

Follow the articulation carefully on this one.

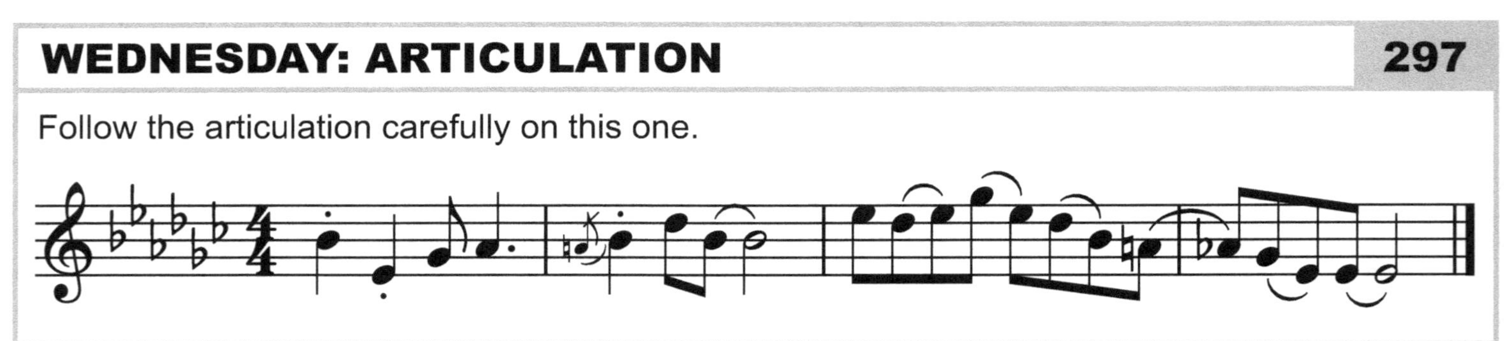

THURSDAY: LONG TONES 298

Here is the A blues scale in long tones:

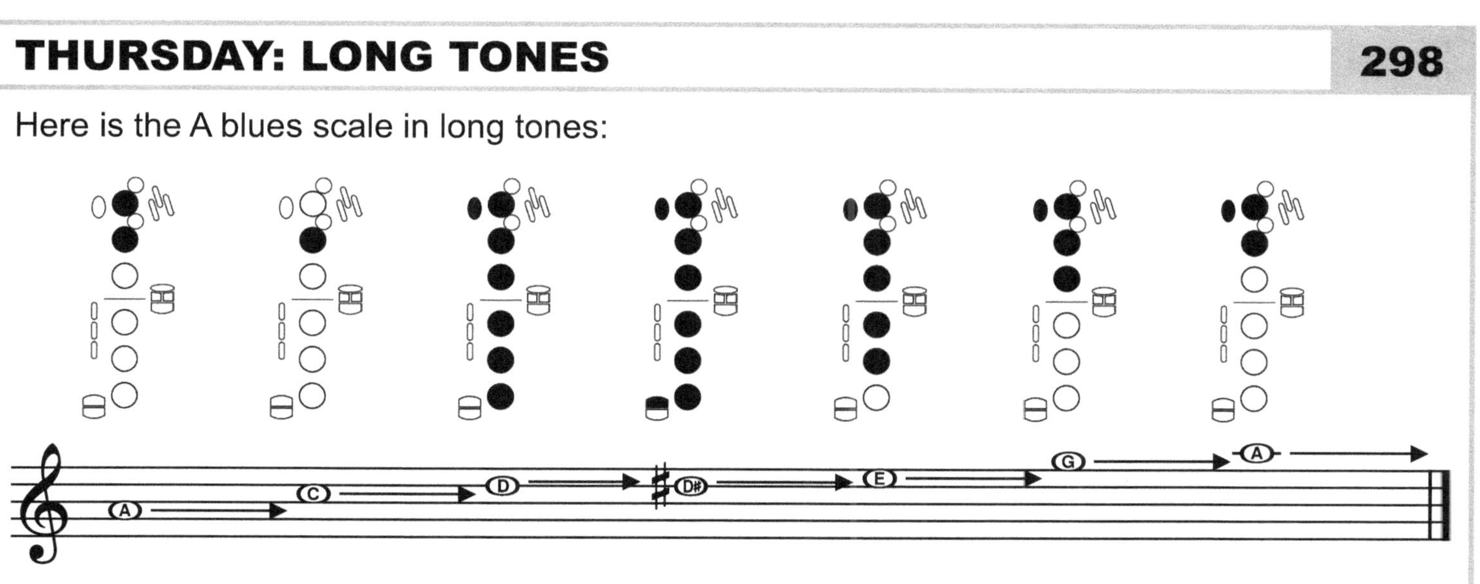

FRIDAY: RHYTHM 299

Listen to the recording and then start slowly on this piece. There are a lot of small nuances.

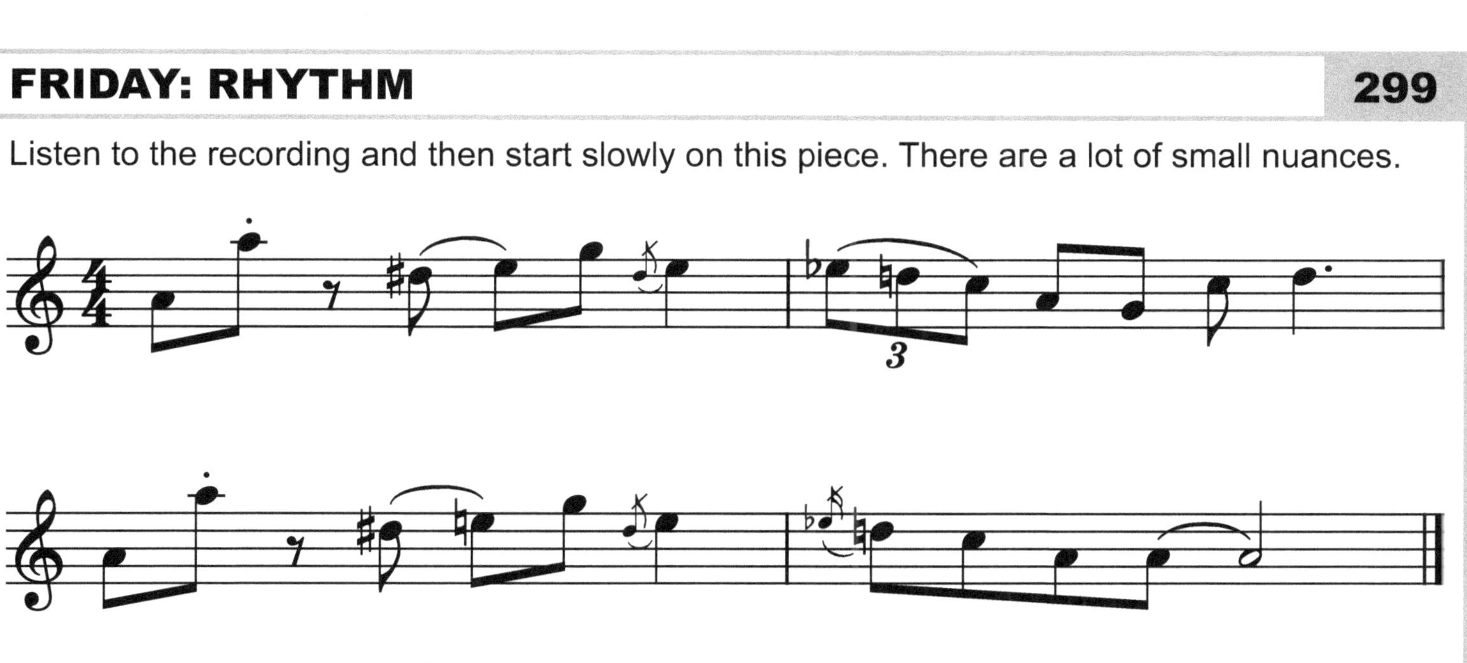

SATURDAY: ARTICULATION 300

This piece is in 3/4 time.

SUNDAY: MUSICAL PIECE

301

The quarter-note tempo of this next piece is slow. However, it sounds fast because it is written in swing 16th notes.

WEEK 44: E & C♯ BLUES SCALES

MONDAY: LONG TONES — 302

This is the E blues scale in long tones.

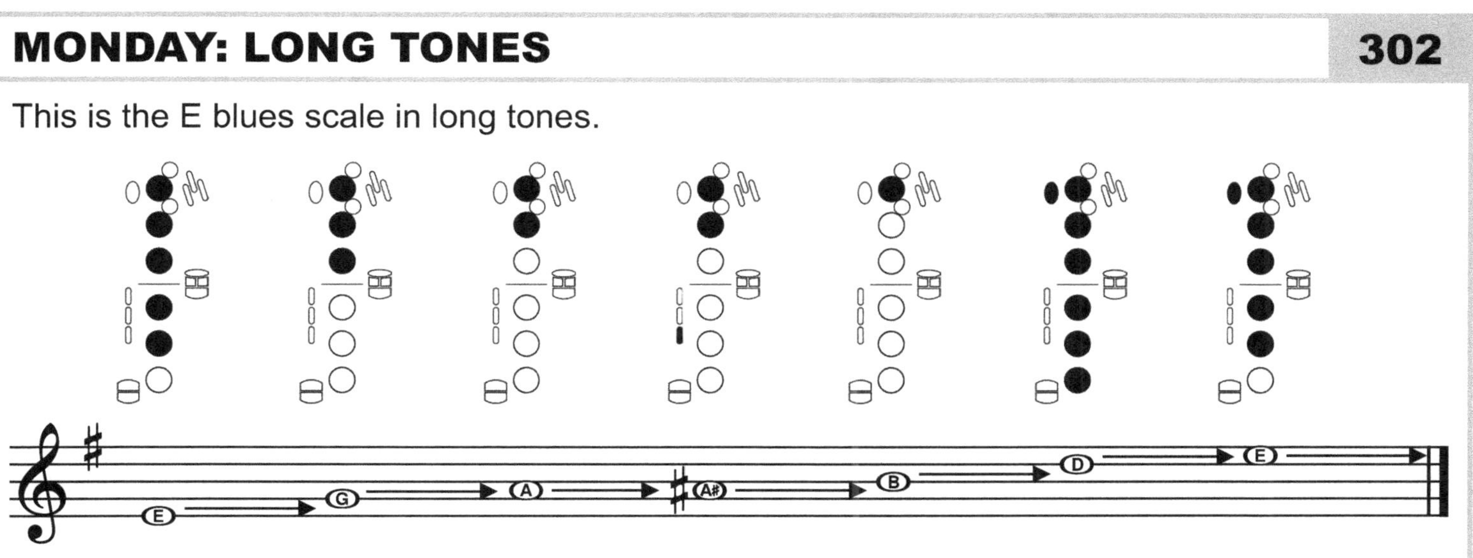

TUESDAY: ARTICULATION — 303

Here's a nice swing piece. The accents will not be written in anymore for swing eighth notes, unless there are special cases. Just listen to the recording and remember that the upbeats generally get a little more emphasis in swing music.

WEDNESDAY: RHYTHM — 304

This piece has some tricky rhythms.

THURSDAY: LONG TONES 305

Here is the C♯ blues scale:

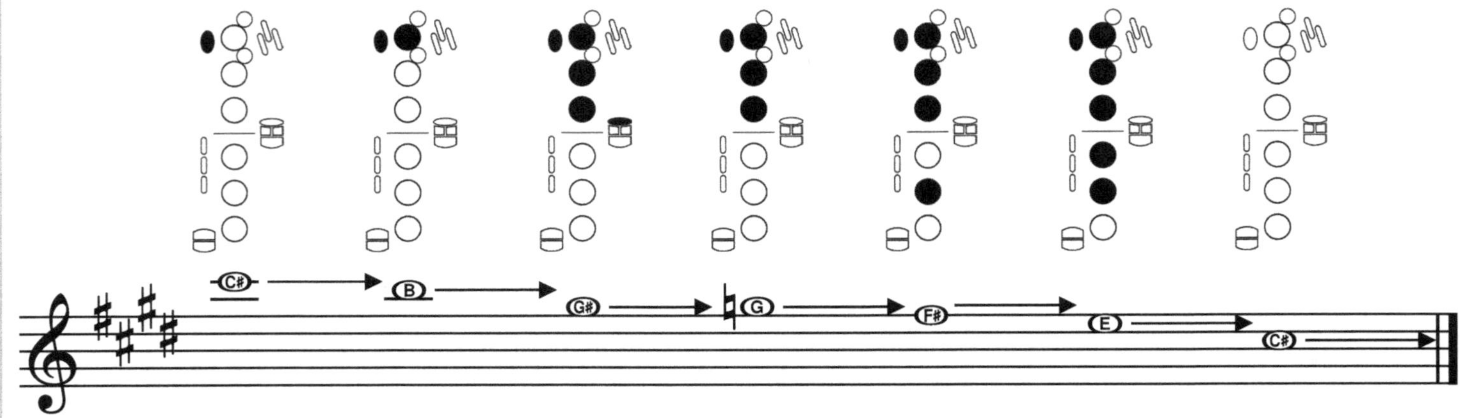

FRIDAY: ARTICULATION 306

Today, you'll learn a new articulation, *fortepiano (fp)*. The attack of the note should be hard and loud, then immediately reduce the volume to *piano*. In this case, there is a crescendo right afterwards that leads into the next note.

SATURDAY: RHYTHM 307

Here is a swing piece in 3/4 time to work on today:

SUNDAY: MUSICAL PIECE 308

There is a *fortepiano* marking in this piece. The crescendo afterwards should bring you back up to the same dynamic level you started at.

WEEK 45: B & F♯ BLUES SCALES

MONDAY: LONG TONES 309

Here is the B blues scale:

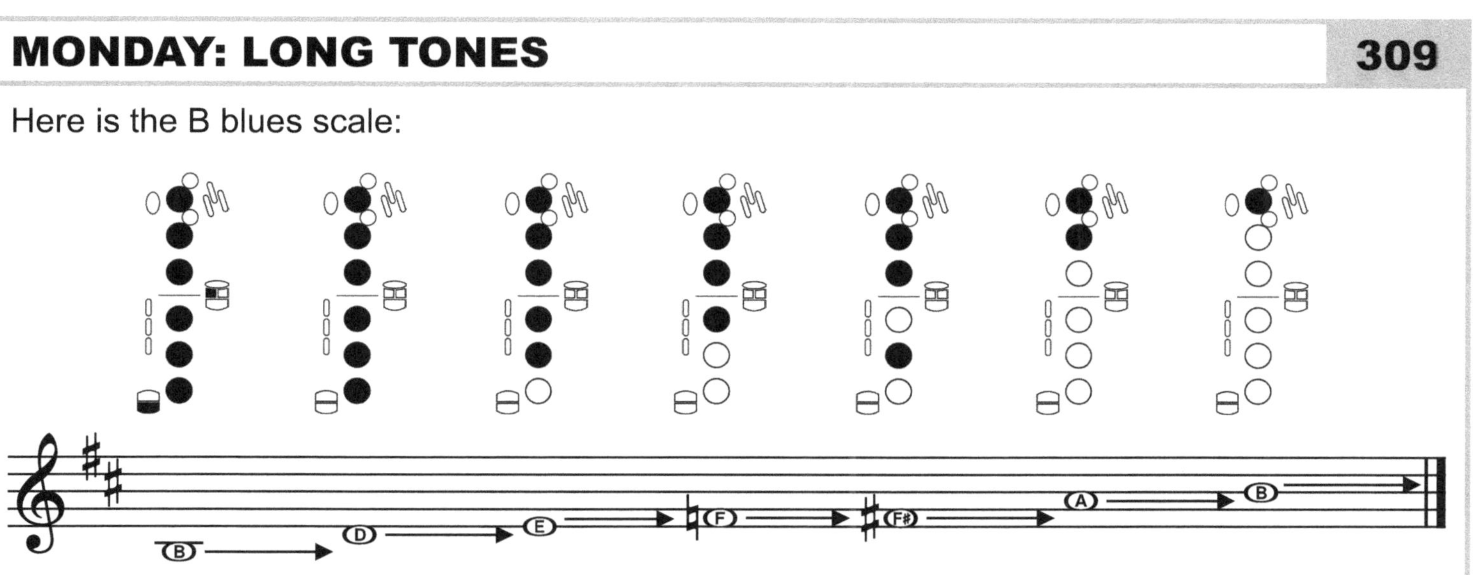

TUESDAY: RHYTHM 310

This piece has a technically difficult passage in bar 3. Try practicing this bar separately for a while at slower tempos before attempting the entire piece. (**Tip:** Use the F-natural to F♯ trill fingering for the 16th-note passage.)

WEDNESDAY: ARTICULATION 311

All the upbeats in the beginning of this piece should be accented and short. The third bar, with its smooth and connected notes, offers a nice contrast to the short notes.

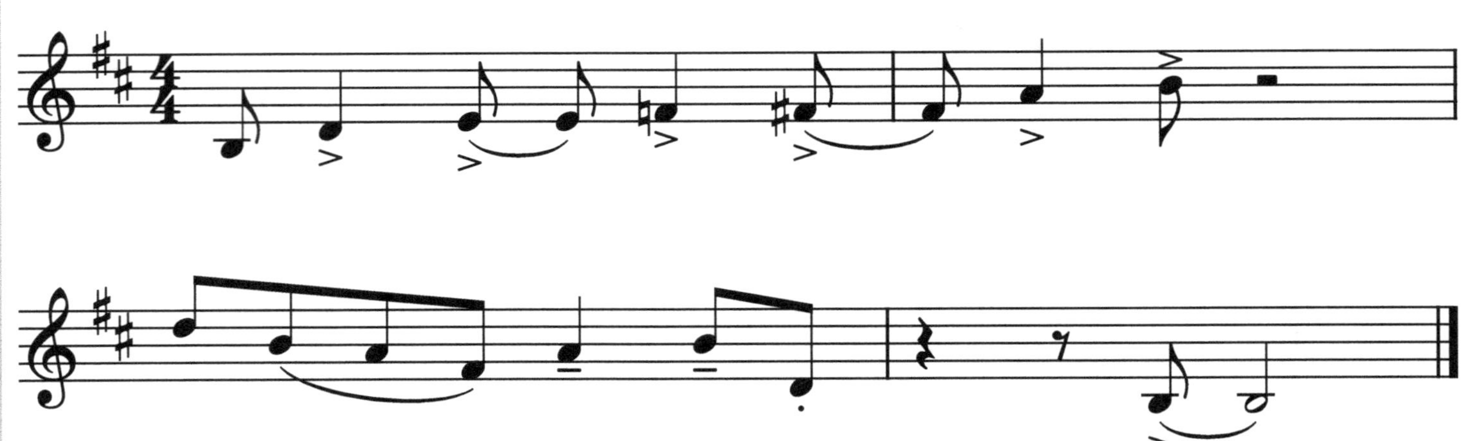

THURSDAY: LONG TONES 312

Here is the F♯ blues scale going down in long tones:

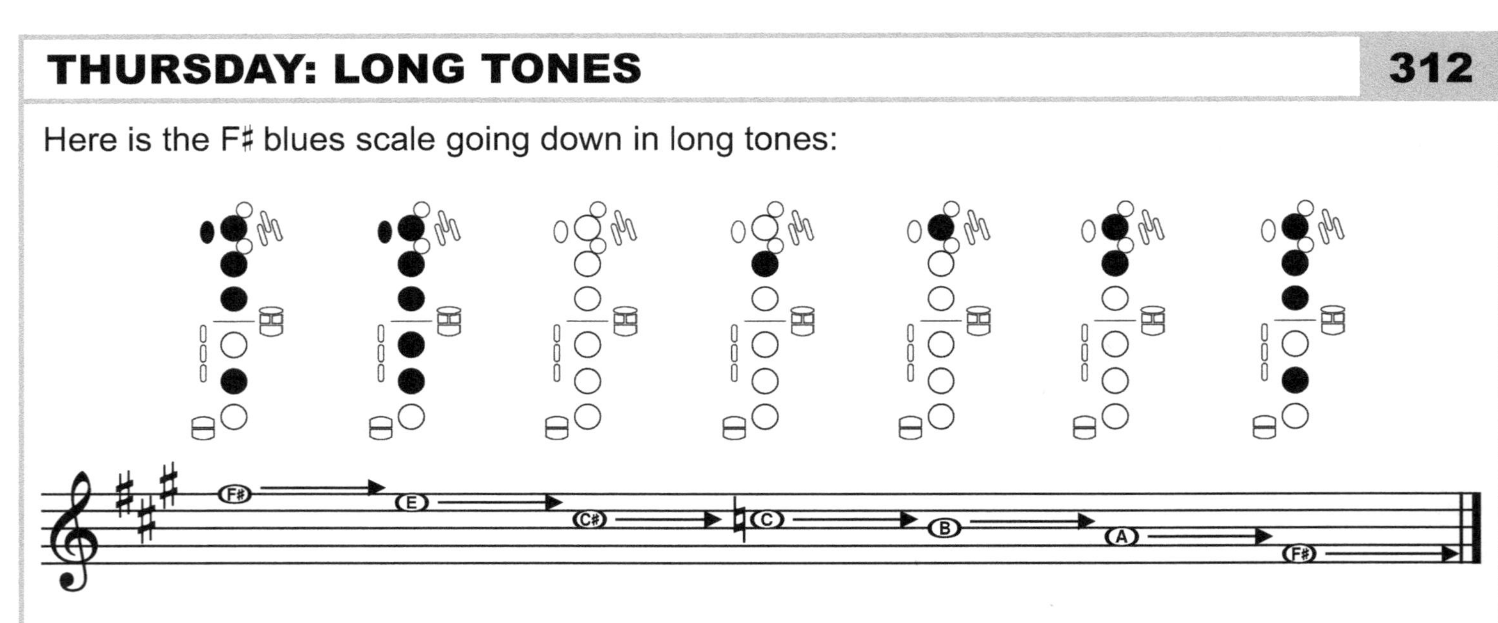

FRIDAY: RHYTHM

313

At this point in the book, you should be ready for a bit of a challenge. Listen to the recording before playing this piece. Some of the rhythmic figures are played in a slightly different swing style from the way they look.

SATURDAY: ARTICULATION

314

Here is a nice, relaxed, relatively easy piece in 3/4 time:

SUNDAY: MUSICAL PIECE

315

You'll find a good deal of syncopation in this piece. For example, the beginning features eighth notes accented in groups of 3.

WEEK 46: C & B♭ MAJOR ii–V–I

MONDAY: LONG TONES 316

For the next six weeks, you'll be working on ii–V–I ("two-five-one") progressions. This is one of the most common chord progressions in jazz music. Today, you'll play the chord tones of these three chords in the key of C major. This may be too many long tones to play in one sitting. If you feel your embouchure getting shaky, take a five-minute break and then continue.

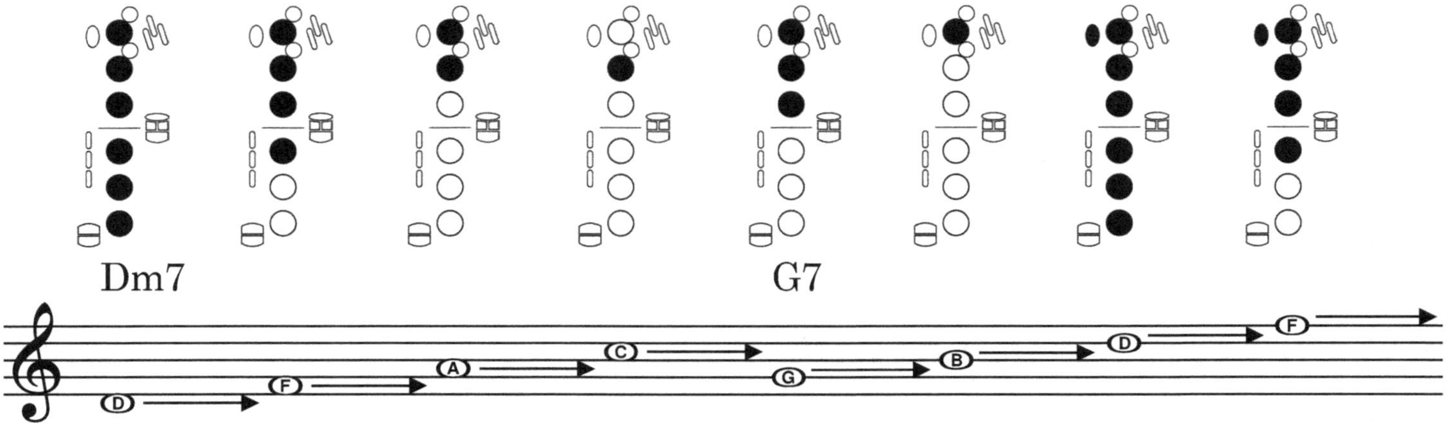

Dm7 G7

D F A C G B D F

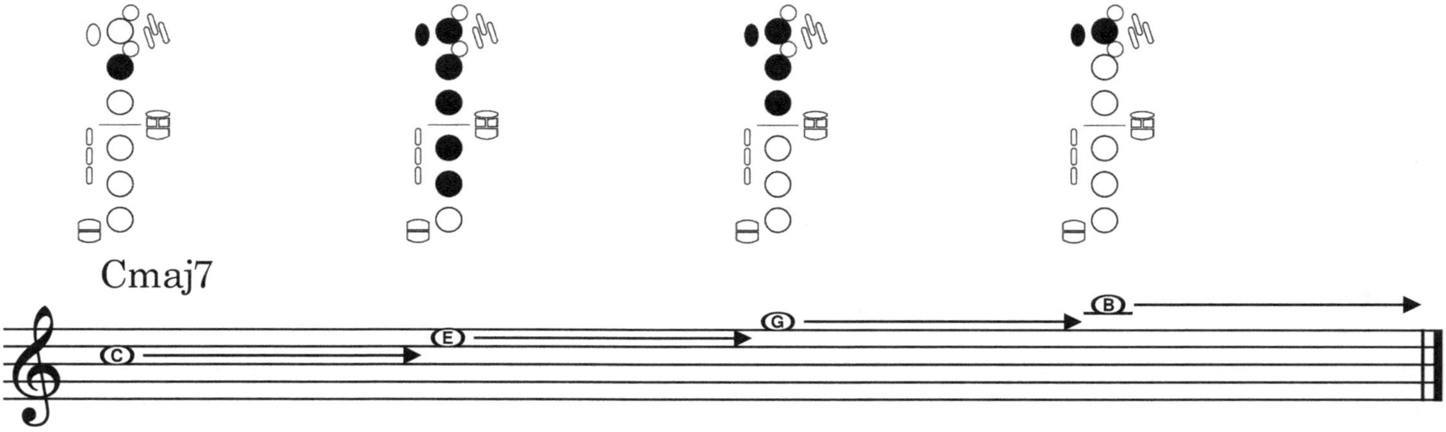

Cmaj7

C E G B

TUESDAY: D DORIAN, G MIXOLYDIAN & C IONIAN 317

Today, you'll play the scales associated with the chords in a C major ii–V–I progression: D Dorian, G Mixolydian, and C Ionian (major).

WEDNESDAY: ii–V–I LICK 318

Here is a short piece written over the ii–V–I progression. This is meant to be played in a swing style; however, I have not written in the articulation. From now on, you'll have to use what you have learned so far in the book to come up with the proper articulation. As always, listen to the recordings to get an idea.

THURSDAY: LONG TONES 319

Here are the chord tones for a ii–V–I progression in B♭. Take breaks when needed.

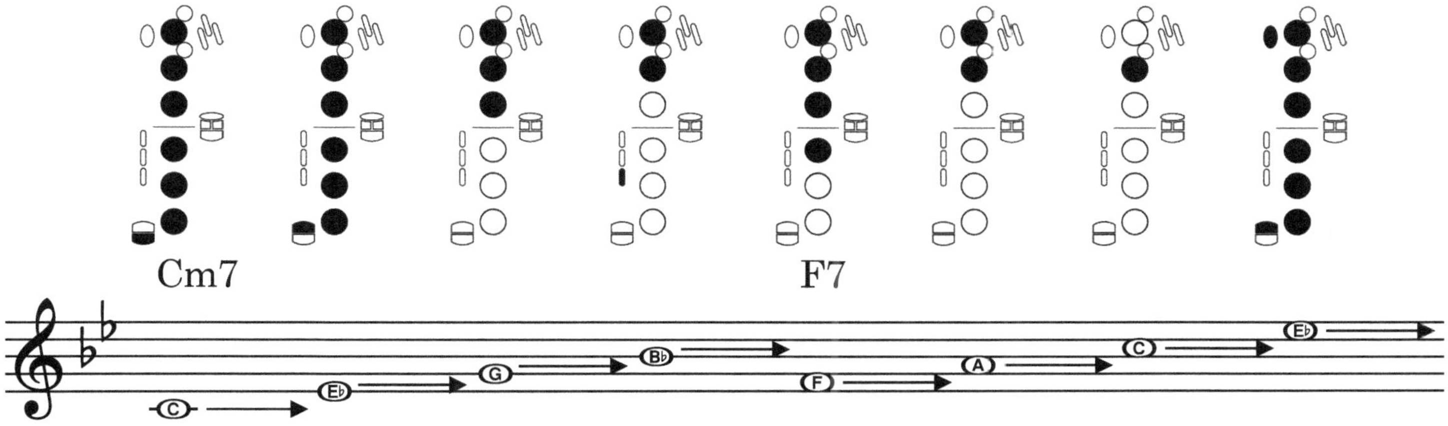

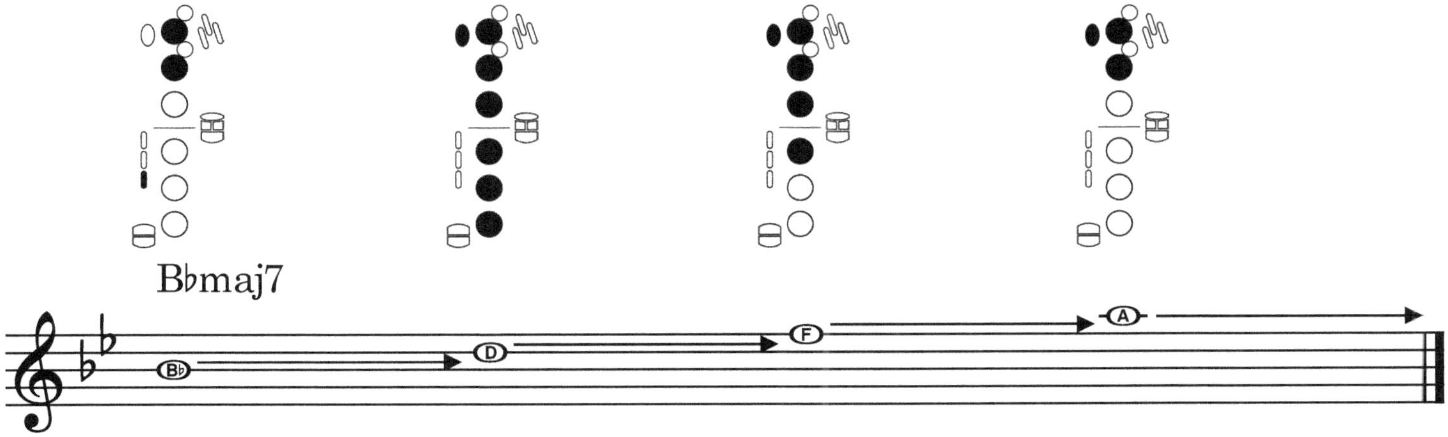

Cm7 F7

C Eb G Bb F A C Eb

B♭maj7

Bb D F A

FRIDAY: C DORIAN, F MIXOLYDIAN & B♭ IONIAN 320

Play these scales with different articulations. Also, try playing them with a swing feel.

SATURDAY: ii–V–I LICK 321

In this lick, each of the first three bars starts with the root, 3rd, and 5th of the chord.

SUNDAY: iii–VI–ii–V–I LICK 322

For the next six Sundays, you'll play a iii–VI–ii–V–I lick incorporating both keys that you worked on for the week. Today, for the first week, you'll play just the chord tones of each chord.

WEEK 47: F & E♭ MAJOR ii–V–I

MONDAY: LONG TONES **323**

Have fun playing your long tones over a ii–V–I chord progression in the key of F major.

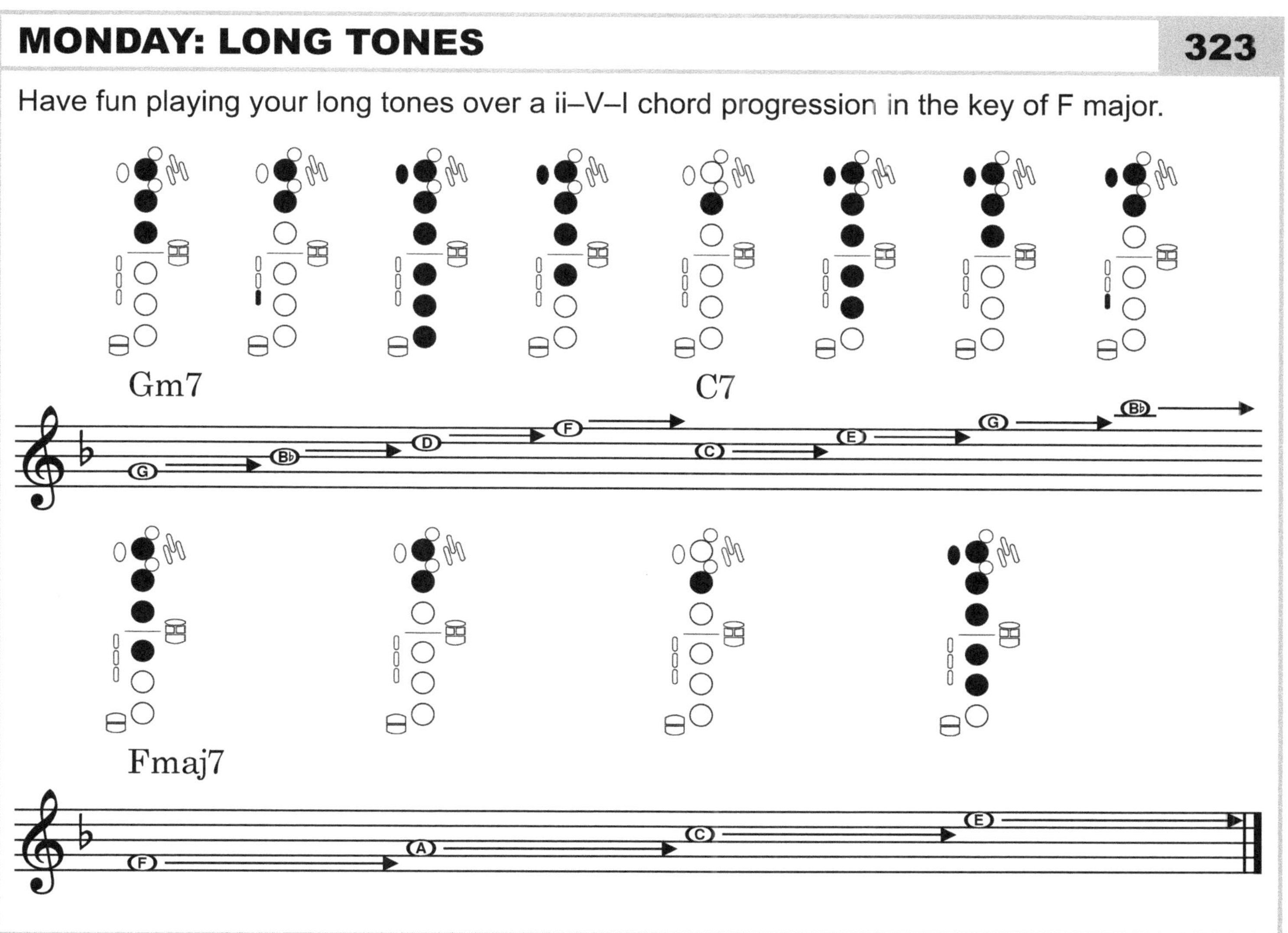

TUESDAY: G DORIAN, C MIXOLYDIAN & F IONIAN **324**

Here are your scales for the ii–V–I progression in F major. Try mixing it up by playing the scales in descending fashion.

Gm7 C7 Fmaj7

WEDNESDAY: ii–V–I LICK

325

In today's ii–V–I lick, you'll notice the use of a passing tone at the end of the first bar to make a smooth transition to the next chord.

Gm7
C7
Fmaj7

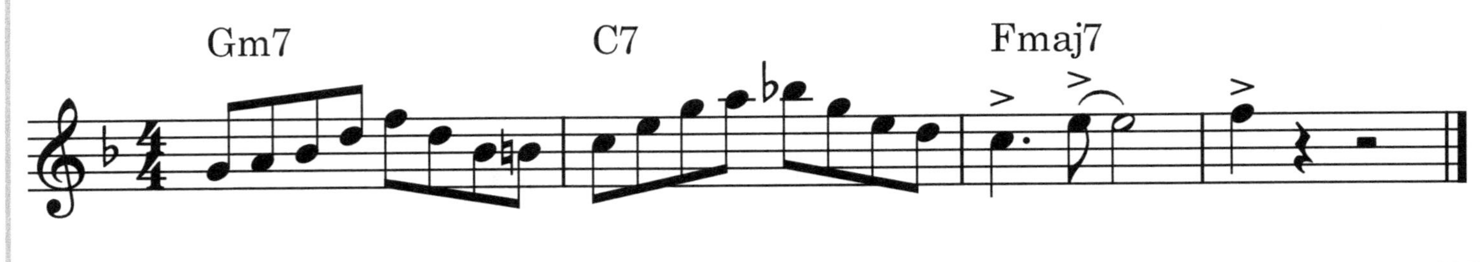

THURSDAY: LONG TONES

326

Here are your ii–V–I long tones in E♭ major:

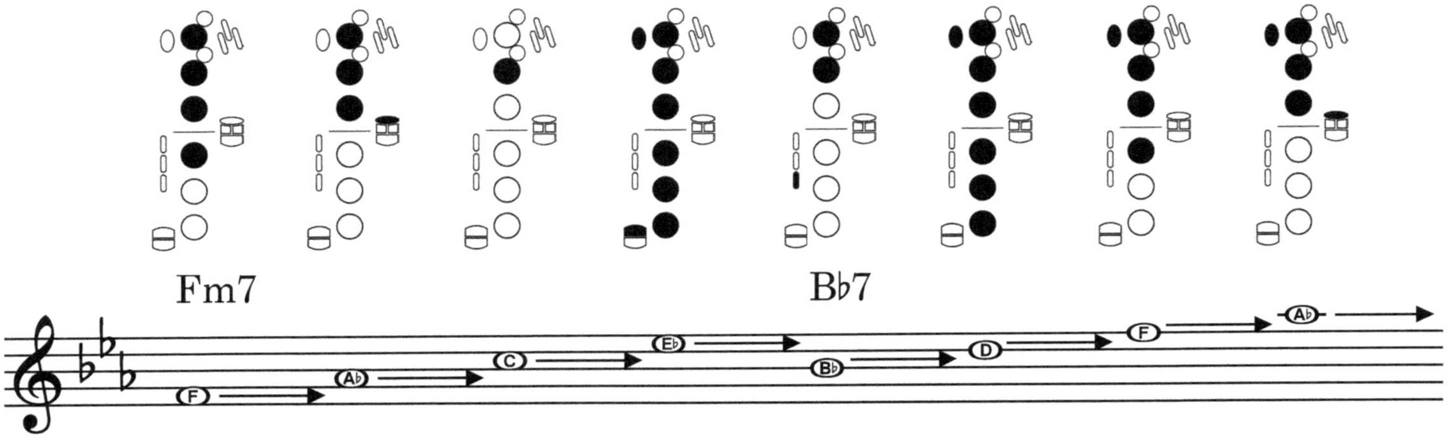

Fm7
B♭7
F
A♭
C
E♭
B♭
D
F
A♭

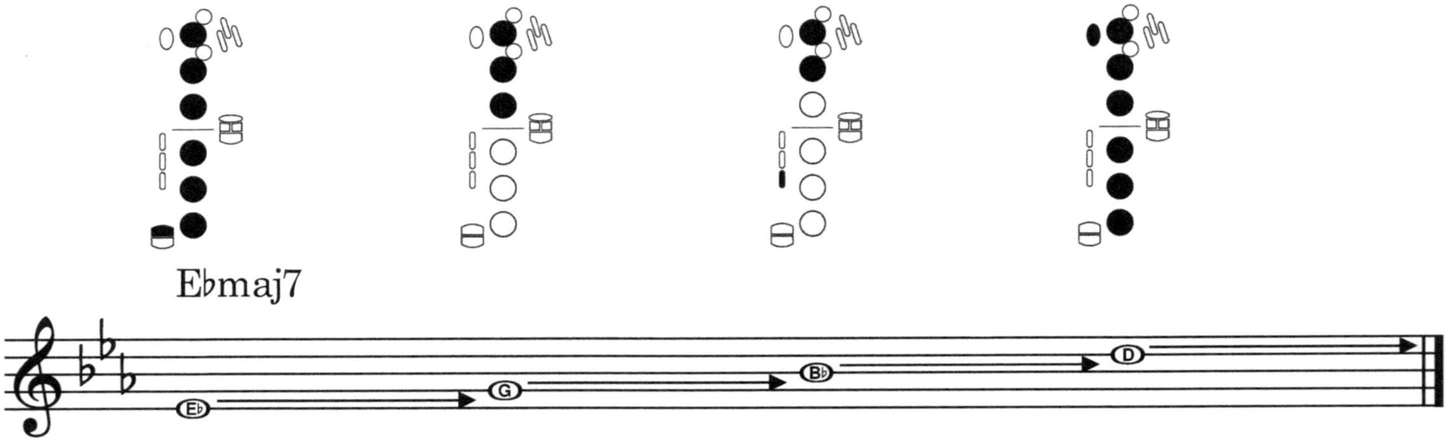

E♭maj7
E♭
G
B♭
D

FRIDAY: F DORIAN, B♭ MIXOLYDIAN & E♭ IONIAN 327

Here are the ii–V–I scales in E♭ major. Try using the "groups of 4" scale pattern from Day 39 to play these scales.

SATURDAY: ii–V–I LICK 328

Here is a piece going through the ii–V–I progression in the key of E♭ major. See if you can identify which notes are chord tones and which notes are passing tones.

SUNDAY: iii–VI–ii–V–I LICK 329

This is your Sunday iii–VI–ii–V–I piece. It's basically a ii–V progression going through both keys you've worked on this week, F major and E♭ major.

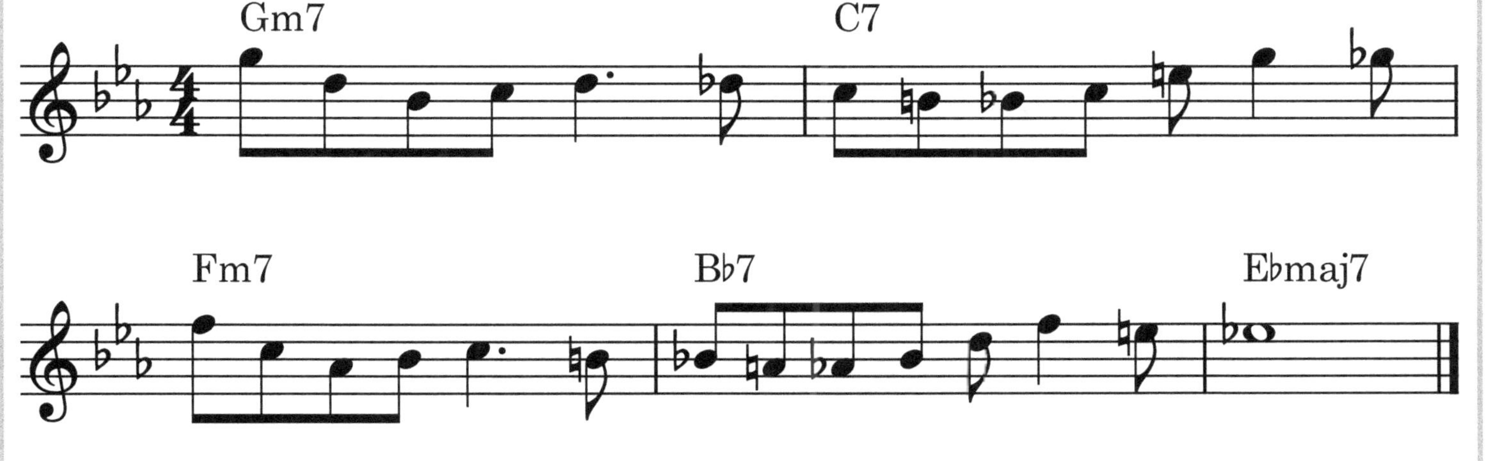

WEEK 48: A & G MAJOR ii–V–I

MONDAY: LONG TONES 330

Here are the chord tones of a ii–V–I progression in the key of A major:

Bm7
E7
B
D
F#
A
E
G#
B
D

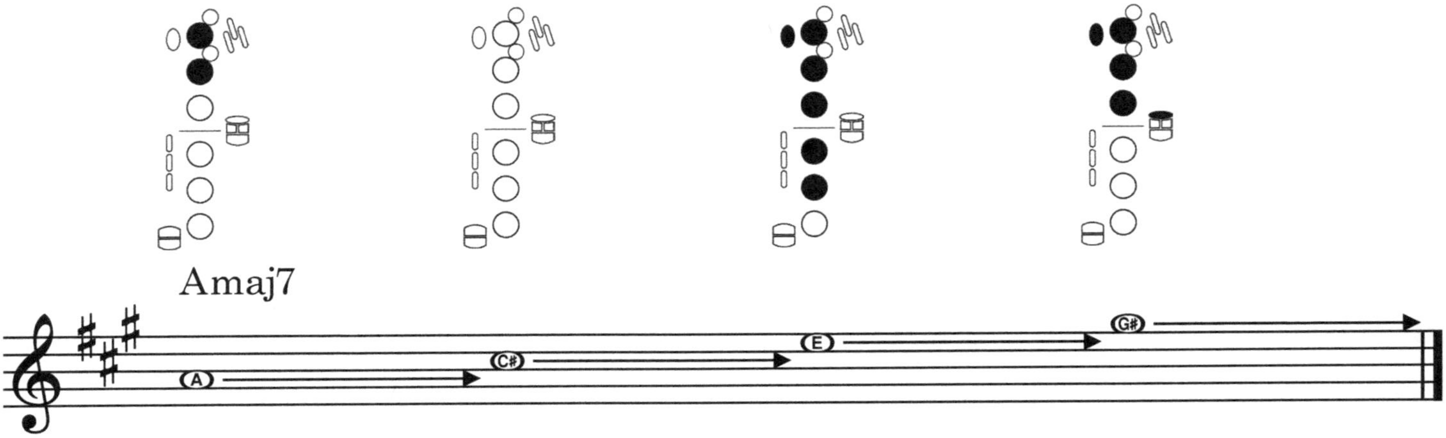

Amaj7
A
C#
E
G#

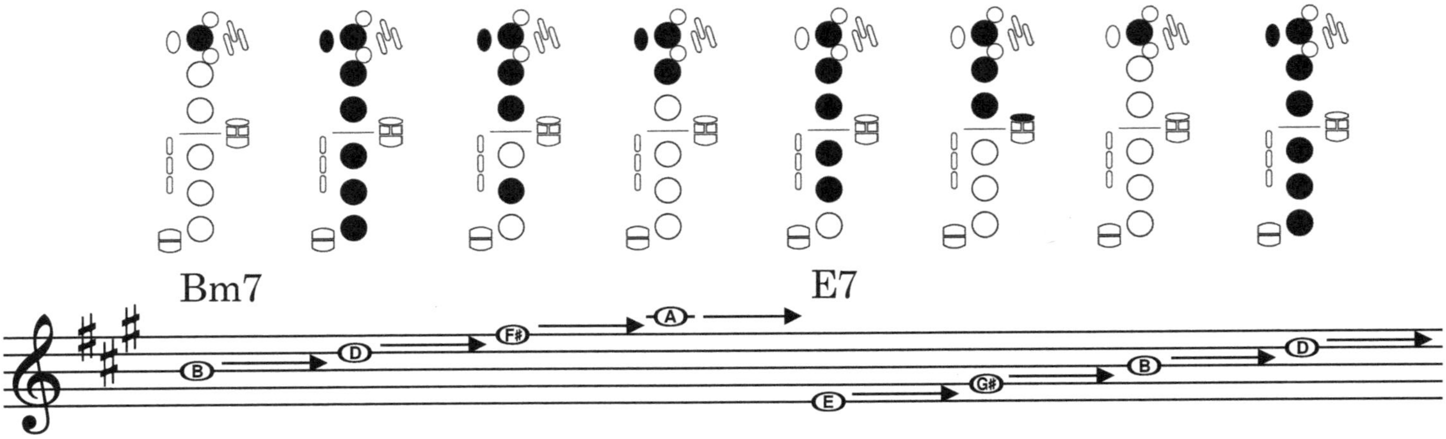

TUESDAY: B DORIAN, E MIXOLYDAN & A IONIAN 331

Here are the scales associated with the ii–V–I progression in the key of A major:

Bm7
E7
Amaj7

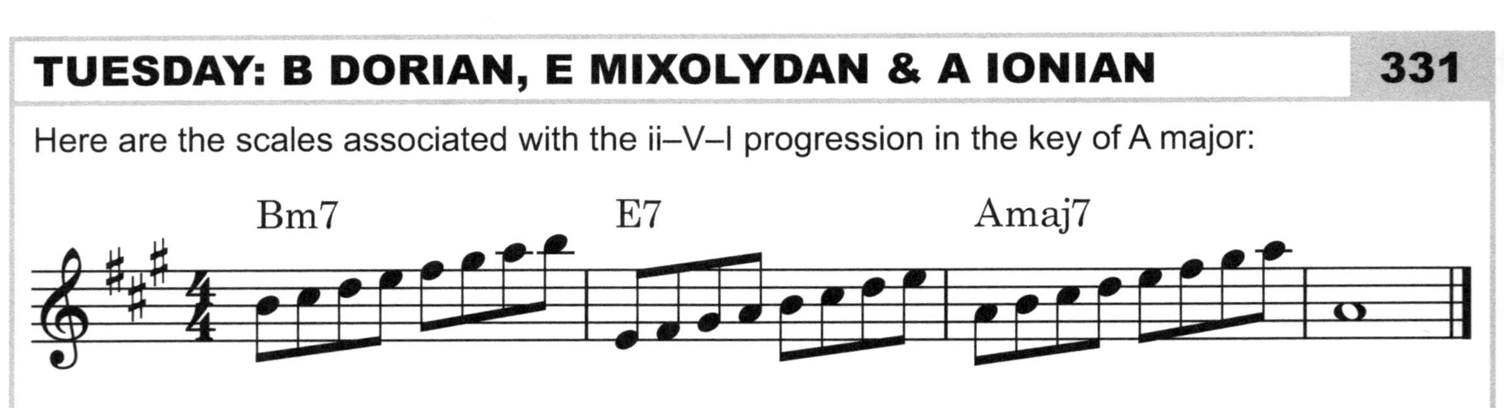

WEDNESDAY: ii–V–I LICK

332

Here's a melody played over the ii–V–I progression in A major. Notice the passing tones in this piece.

Bm7
E7
Amaj7

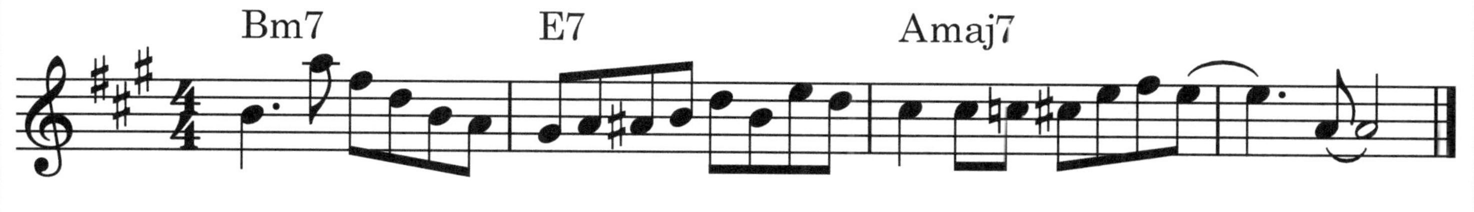

THURSDAY: LONG TONES

333

Here are the chord tones of a ii–V–I progression in the key of G major. As always, take a break in the middle if you feel your embouchure starting to get tired.

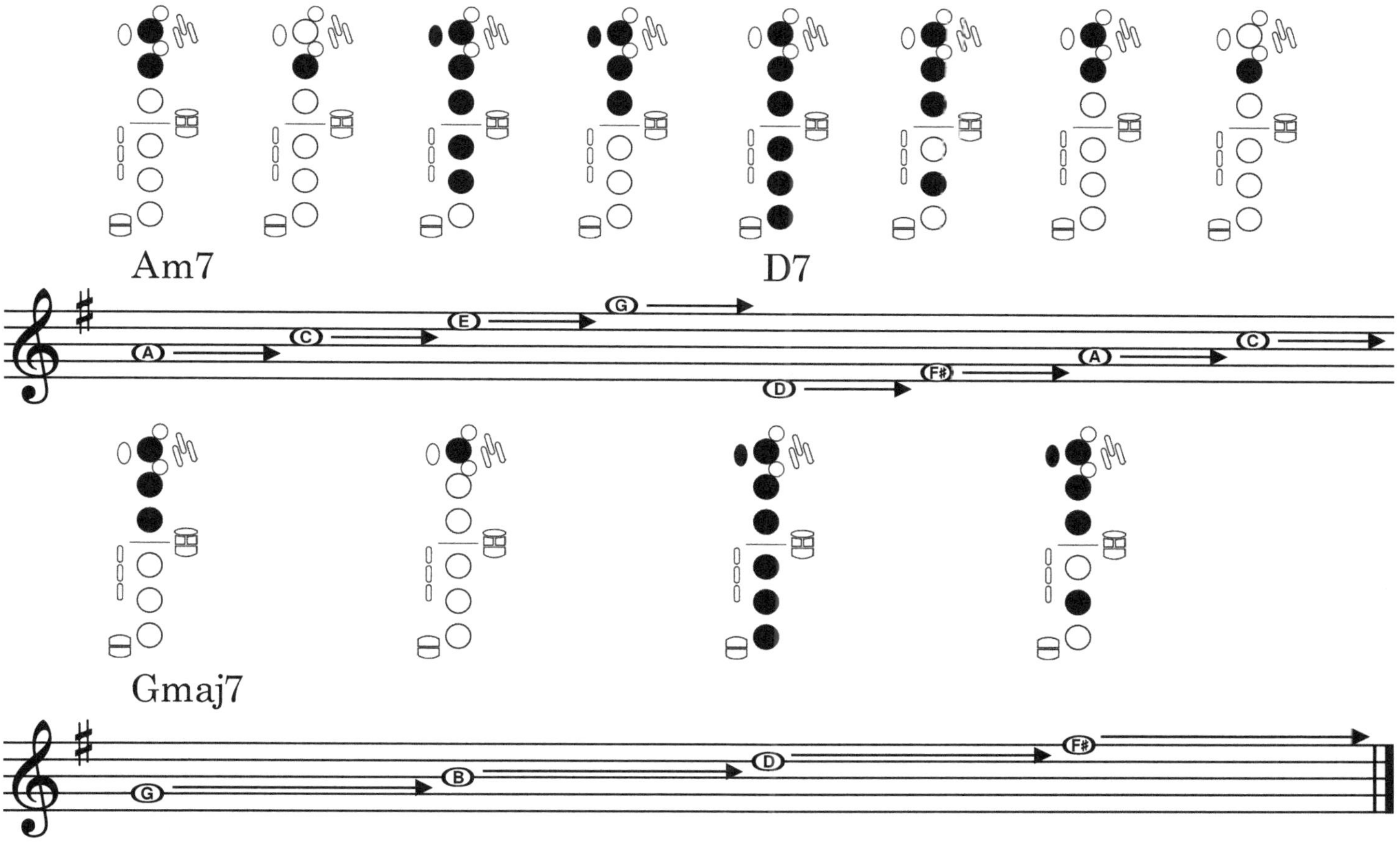
Am7
A
C
E
G
D7
D
F#
A
C
Gmaj7
G
B
D
F#

FRIDAY: A DORIAN, D MIXOLYDIAN & G IONIAN 334

The scales associated with the ii–V–I progression in the key of G major are A Dorian, D Mixolydian, and G Ionian.

SATURDAY: ii–V–I LICK 335

The first half of this piece contains scales, and the second half contains chord tones with lower chromatic passing tones.

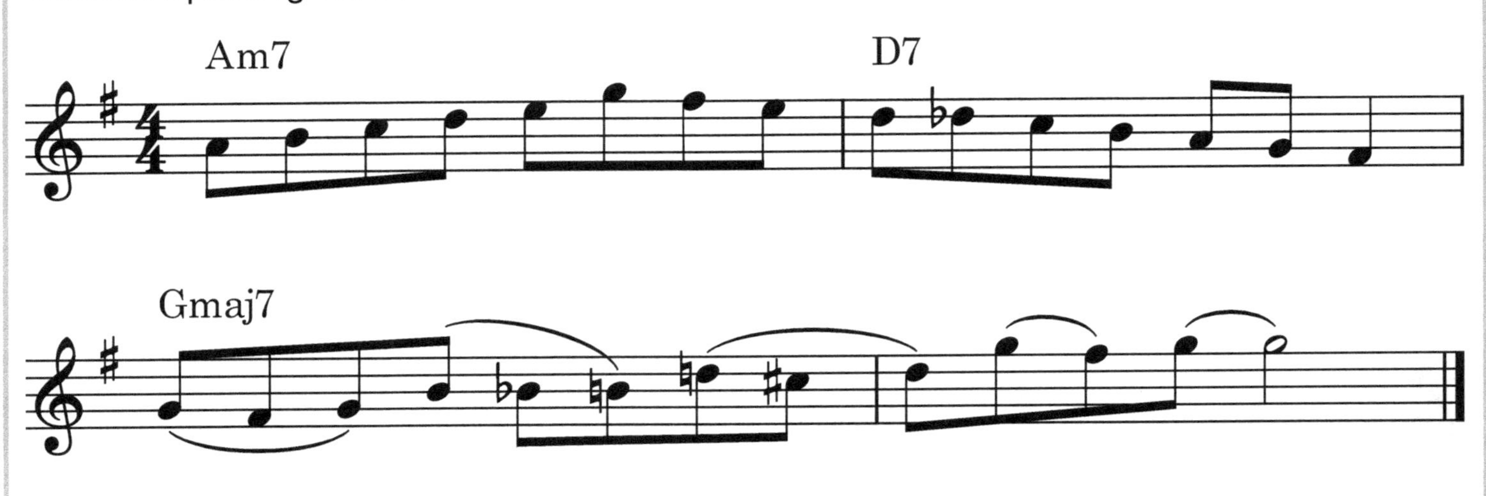

SUNDAY: iii–VI–ii–V–I LICK 336

Enjoy this iii–VI–ii–V–I lick. If you have extra time, try playing it in all 12 keys.

WEEK 49: E & D MAJOR ii–V–I

MONDAY: LONG TONES — 337

Here are the chord tones of a ii–V–I progression in the key of E major:

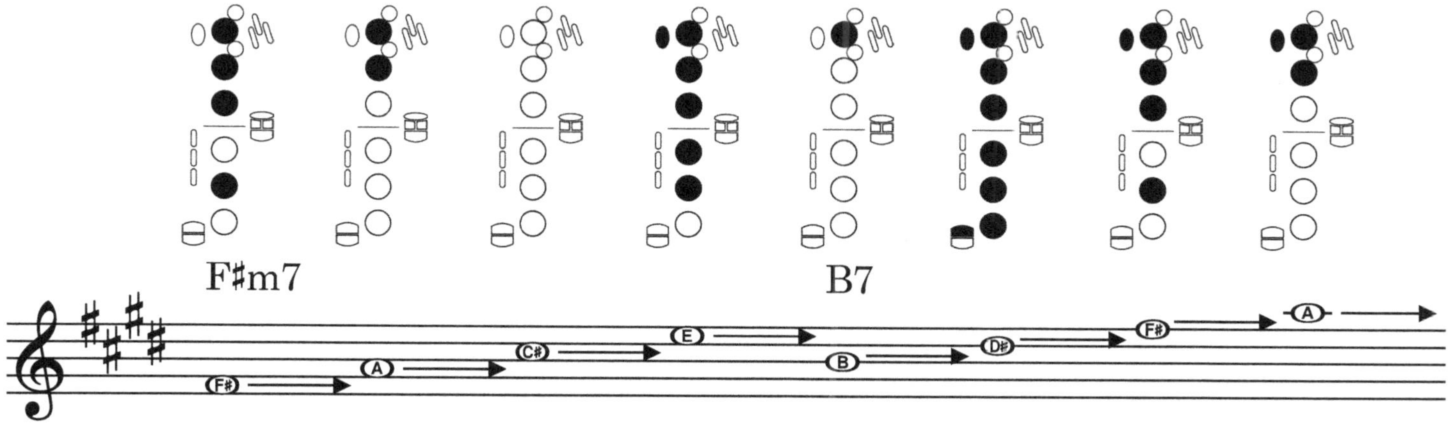
F♯m7
B7
F#
A
C#
E
B
D#
F#
A

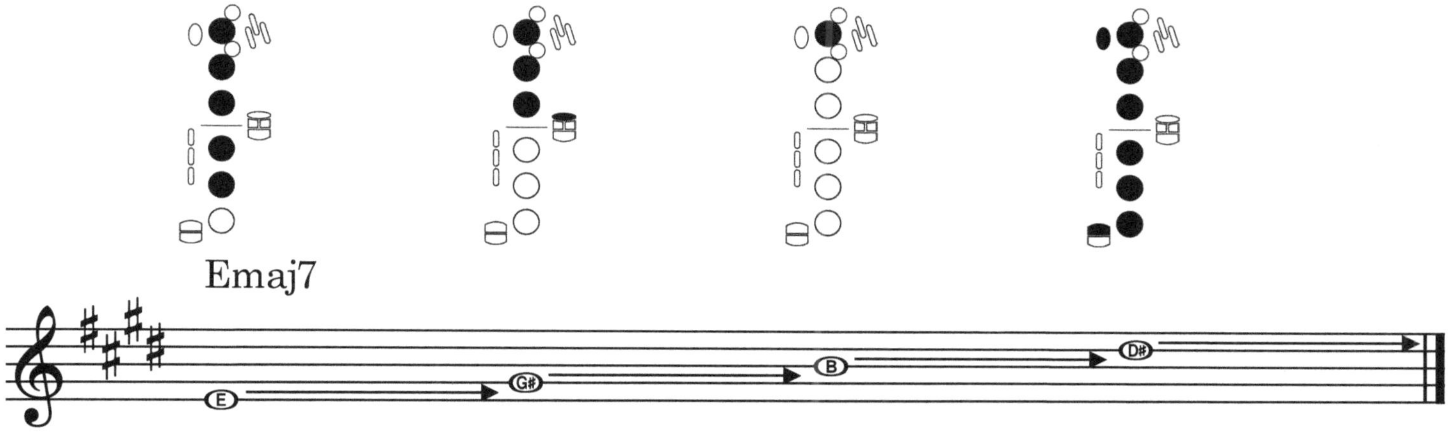
Emaj7
E
G#
B
D#

TUESDAY: F♯ DORIAN, B MIXOLYDIAN & E IONIAN — 338

Play these scales with different articulations. You could also try playing them in descending fashion.

F♯m7
B7
Emaj7

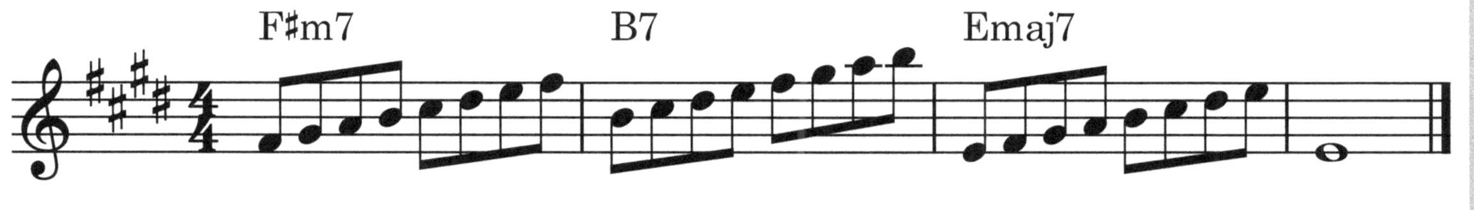

WEDNESDAY: ii–V–I LICK

339

This piece should be played in a laid-back swing style. Listen to the recording to get an idea of the correct articulation.

F♯m7
B7
Emaj7

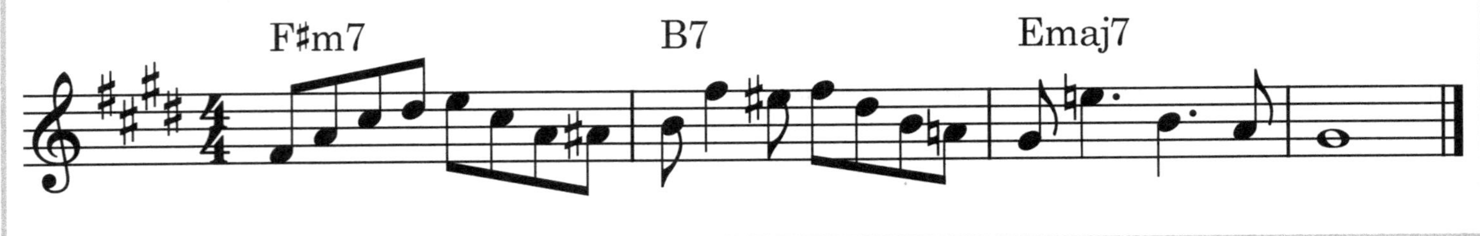

THURSDAY: LONG TONES

340

Here are long tones of the ii–V–I progression in D Major:

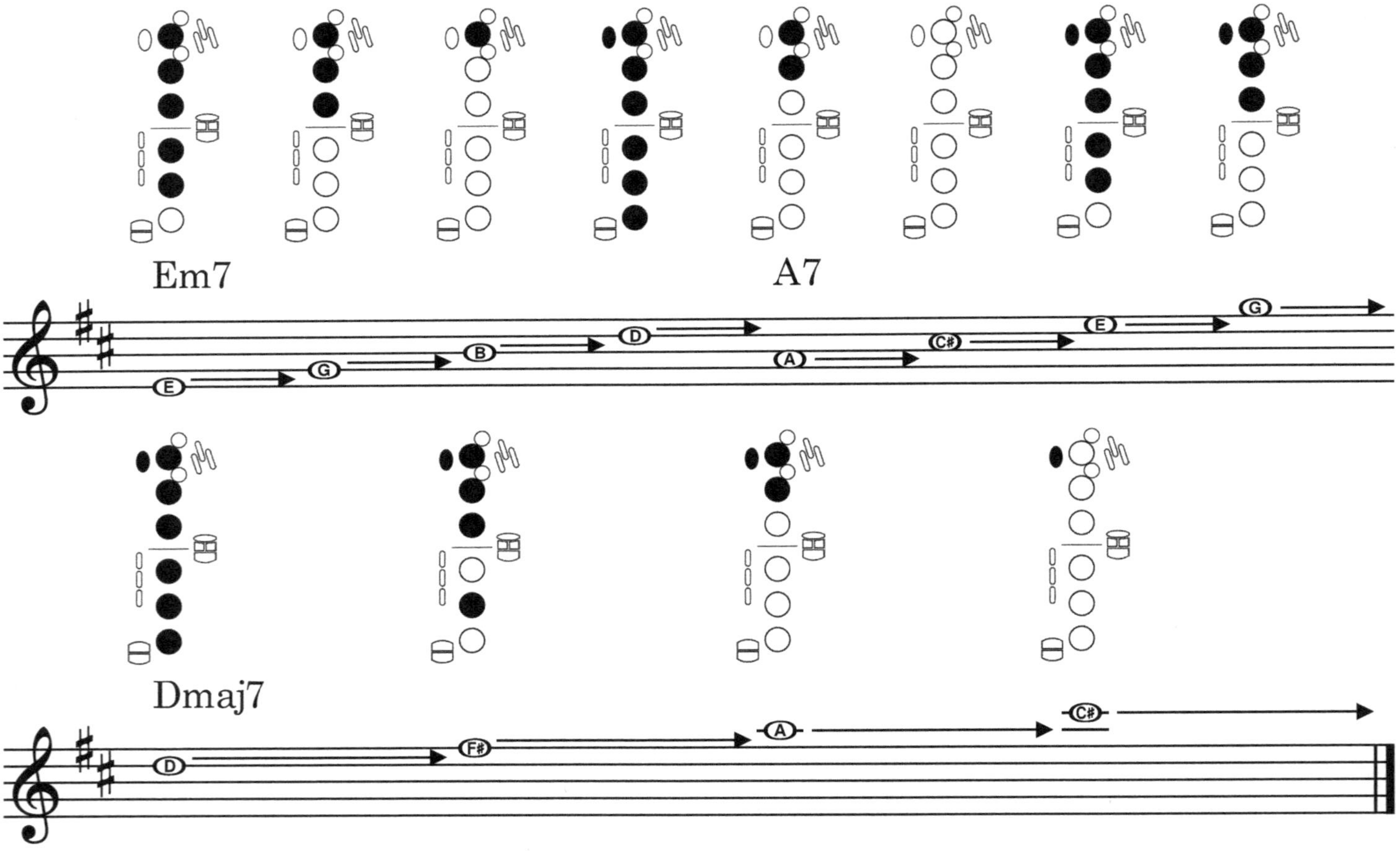

Em7
E
G
B
D
A7
A
C#
E
G
Dmaj7
D
F#
A
C#

FRIDAY: E DORIAN, A MIXOLYDIAN & D IONIAN 341

You can use some of the scale patterns from technique days earlier in this book with the scales in this exercise.

SATURDAY: ii–V–I LICK 342

Try to determine which notes in this piece should be emphasized more than others and then listen to the recording to hear if you are correct.

SUNDAY: iii–VI–ii–V–I LICK 343

This iii–VI–ii–V–I lick uses the passing tone between the root and the ♭7th, which is borrowed from the bebop dominant scale.

WEEK 50: C♯ & B MAJOR ii–V–I

MONDAY: LONG TONES 344

Here are your long tones for the day. This is a ii–V–I progression in the key of C♯ major.

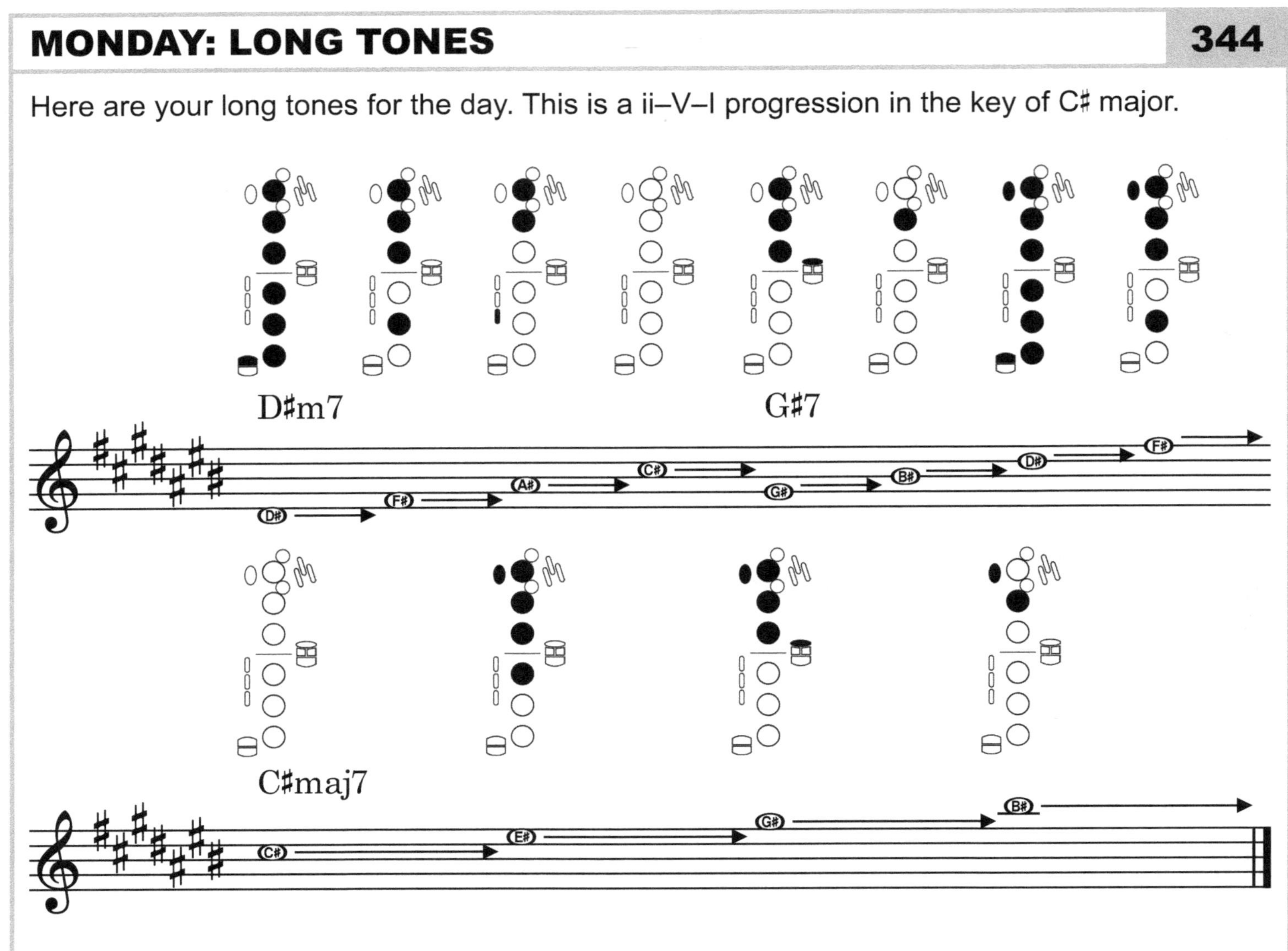

TUESDAY: D♯ DORIAN, G♯ MIXOLYDIAN & C♯ IONIAN 345

As always, mix up the tempos and the articulation of these scales. You could also try playing them at different dynamic levels.

D♯m7 G♯7 C♯maj7

WEDNESDAY: ii–V–I LICK

346

Don't forget about the B♯ in the key signature of this one.

D♯m7
G♯7
C♯maj7

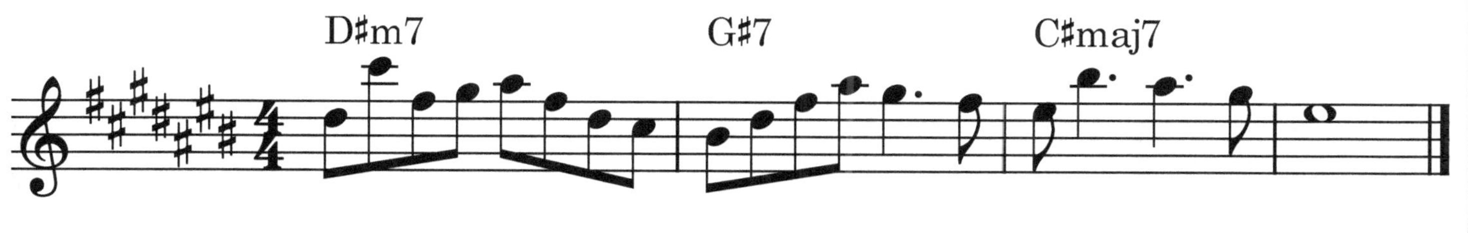

THURSDAY: LONG TONES

347

After you've played your long tones for the day, try making up your own melodies by going through this set of chord changes and using these chord tones.

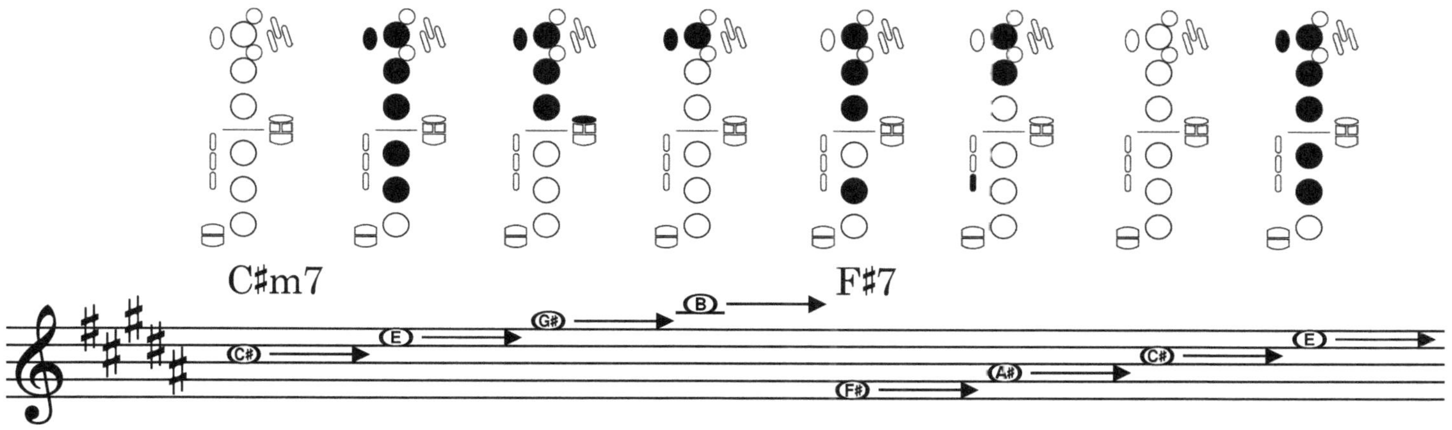

C♯m7
C♯
E
G♯
B
F♯7
F♯
A♯
C♯
E

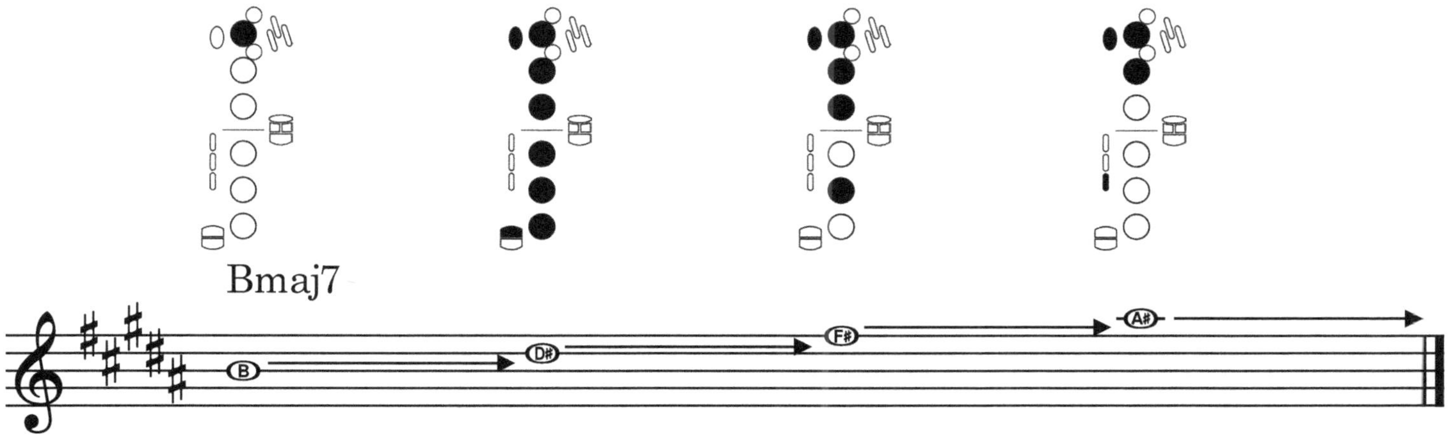

Bmaj7
B
D♯
F♯
A♯

FRIDAY: C♯ DORIAN, F♯ MIXOLYDIAN & B IONIAN — 348

Same thing as yesterday: try to improvise your own melodies by going through this set of chord changes and using these scales.

SATURDAY: ii–V–I LICK — 349

This piece contains interesting passing tones that you could use in your own improvisations.

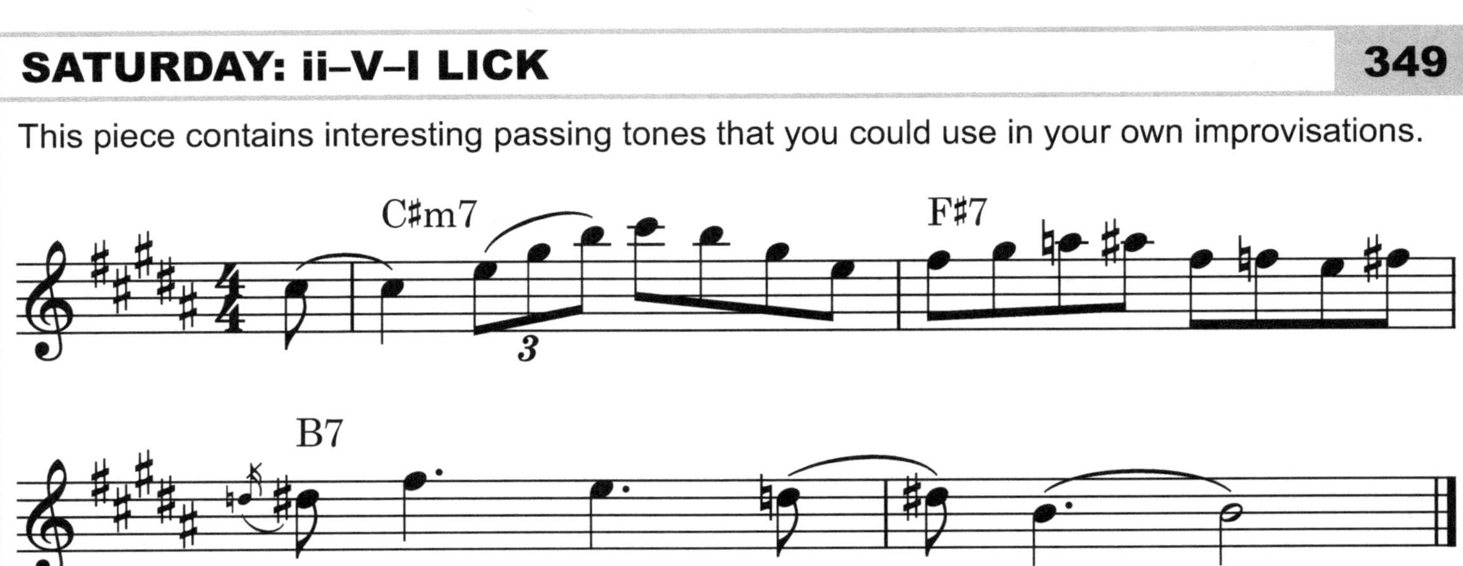

SUNDAY: iii–VI–ii–V–I LICK — 350

This iii–VI–ii–V–I lick mostly consists of chord tones.

WEEK 51: A♭ & F♯ MAJOR ii–V–I

MONDAY: LONG TONES — 351

You've made it to Week 51! Only two more to go! This will be your last week of ii–V–I licks. Next week will be a review of the material you've practiced throughout your journey through this book.

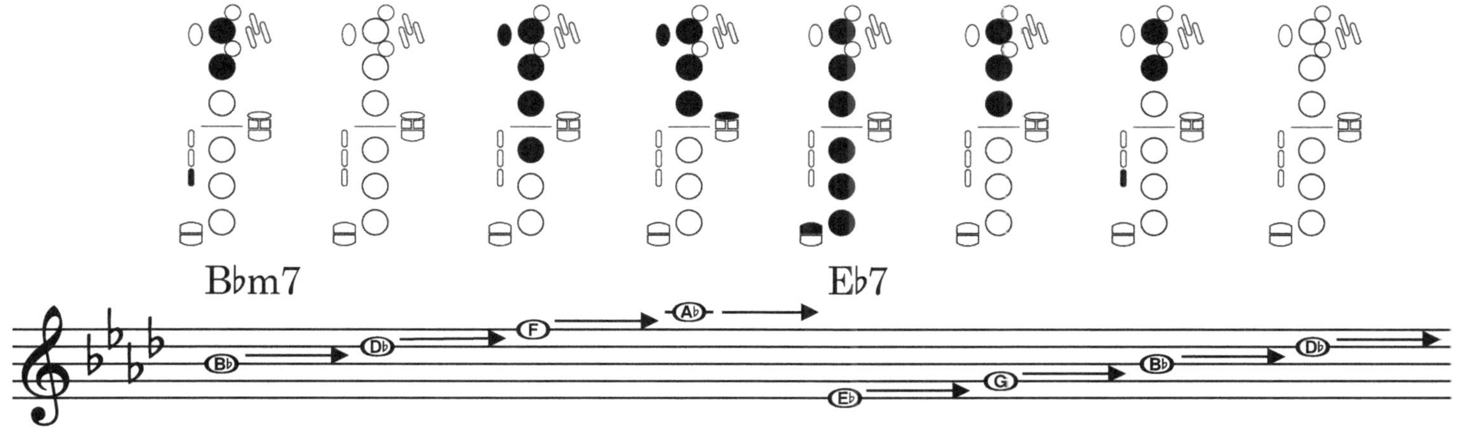

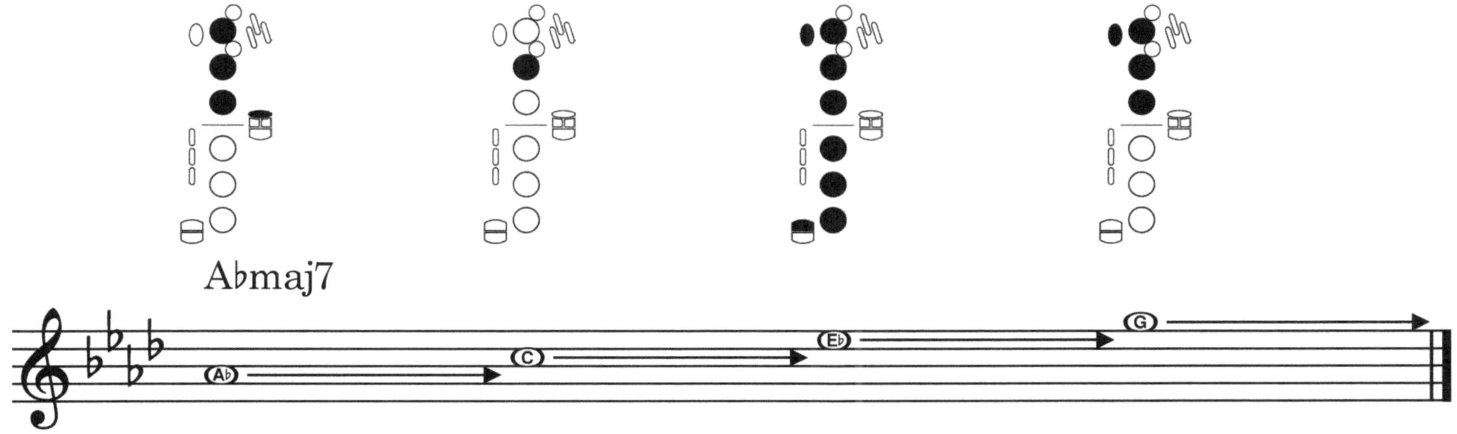

B♭m7
E♭7
B♭
D♭
F
A♭
E♭
G
B♭
D♭

A♭maj7
A♭
C
E♭
G

TUESDAY: B♭ DORIAN, E♭ MIXOLYDIAN & A♭ IONIAN — 352

Here are the scales of a ii–V–I progression in the key of A♭ major:

B♭m7
E♭7
A♭maj7

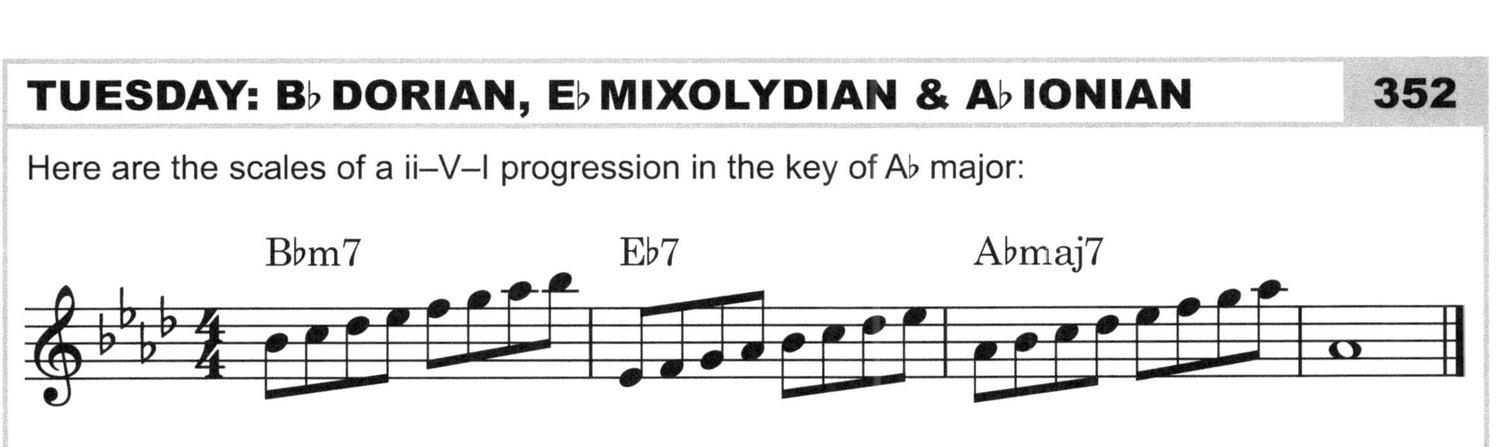

WEDNESDAY: ii–V–I LICK

353

In this piece, you should use the jazz articulation that you've learned earlier in this book.

Bbm7
Eb7
Abmaj7

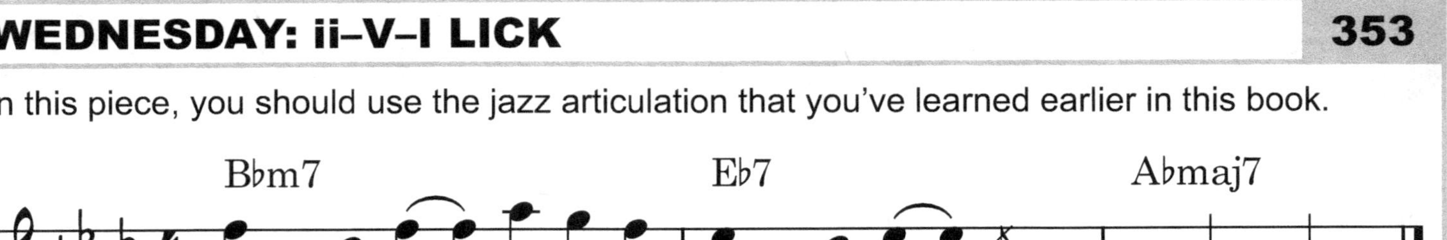

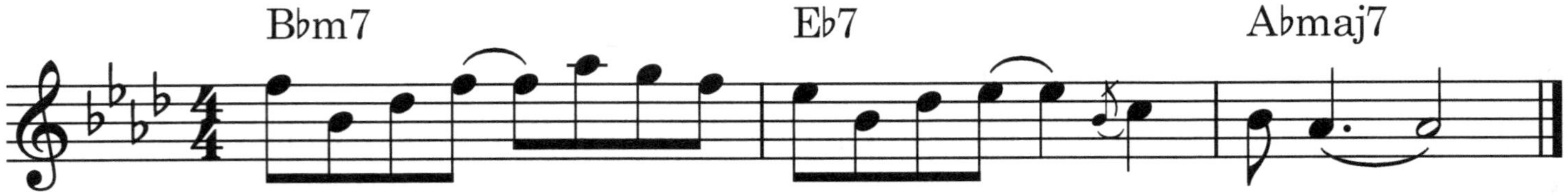

THURSDAY: LONG TONES

354

Here are your long tones in the key of F♯ major:

G♯m7
C♯7
G♯
B
D♯
F♯
C♯
E♯
G♯
B
F♯maj7
F♯
A♯
C♯
E♯

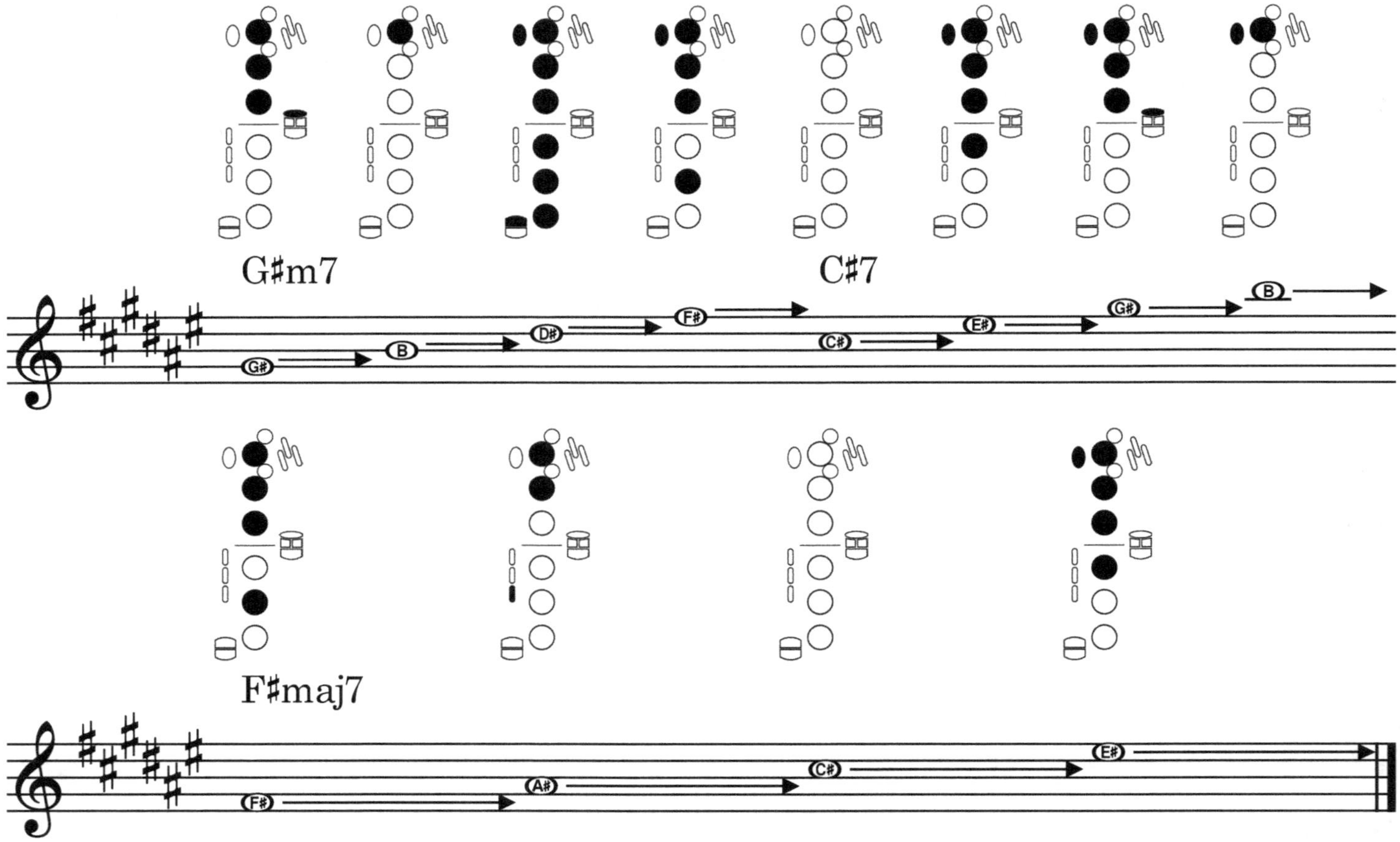

FRIDAY: G♯ DORIAN, C♯ MIXOLYDIAN & F♯ IONIAN — 355

After you practice the scales today, try improvising with them.

SATURDAY: ii–V–I LICK — 356

Specific articulation is notated in the second bar of this piece.

SUNDAY: iii–VI–ii–V–I LICK — 357

See what kind of articulations you can come up with over the triplets in this pattern before listening to the recording. There is no right or wrong approach—sometimes people play the same music with different articulations.

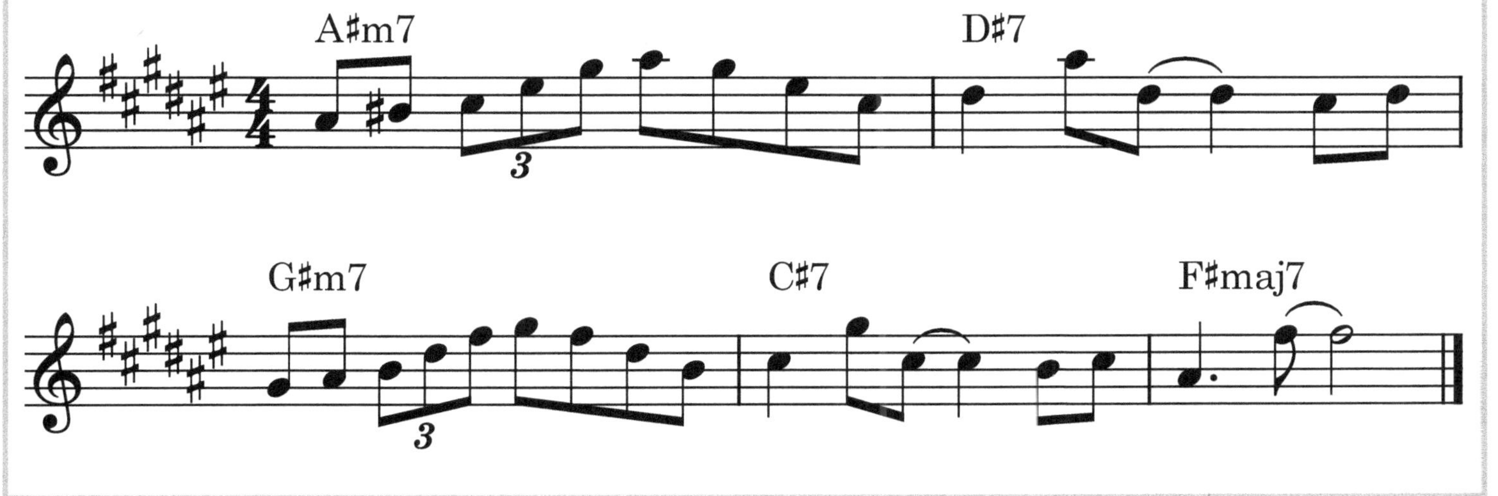

WEEK 52: REVIEW 4

MONDAY: LONG TONES 358

This is your last week! I hope you've enjoyed working in this book. I've really enjoyed writing and organizing it in a way that I thought would be useful. Finish out strong and have a good last week! Here are long tones for you to play over the chromatic scale:

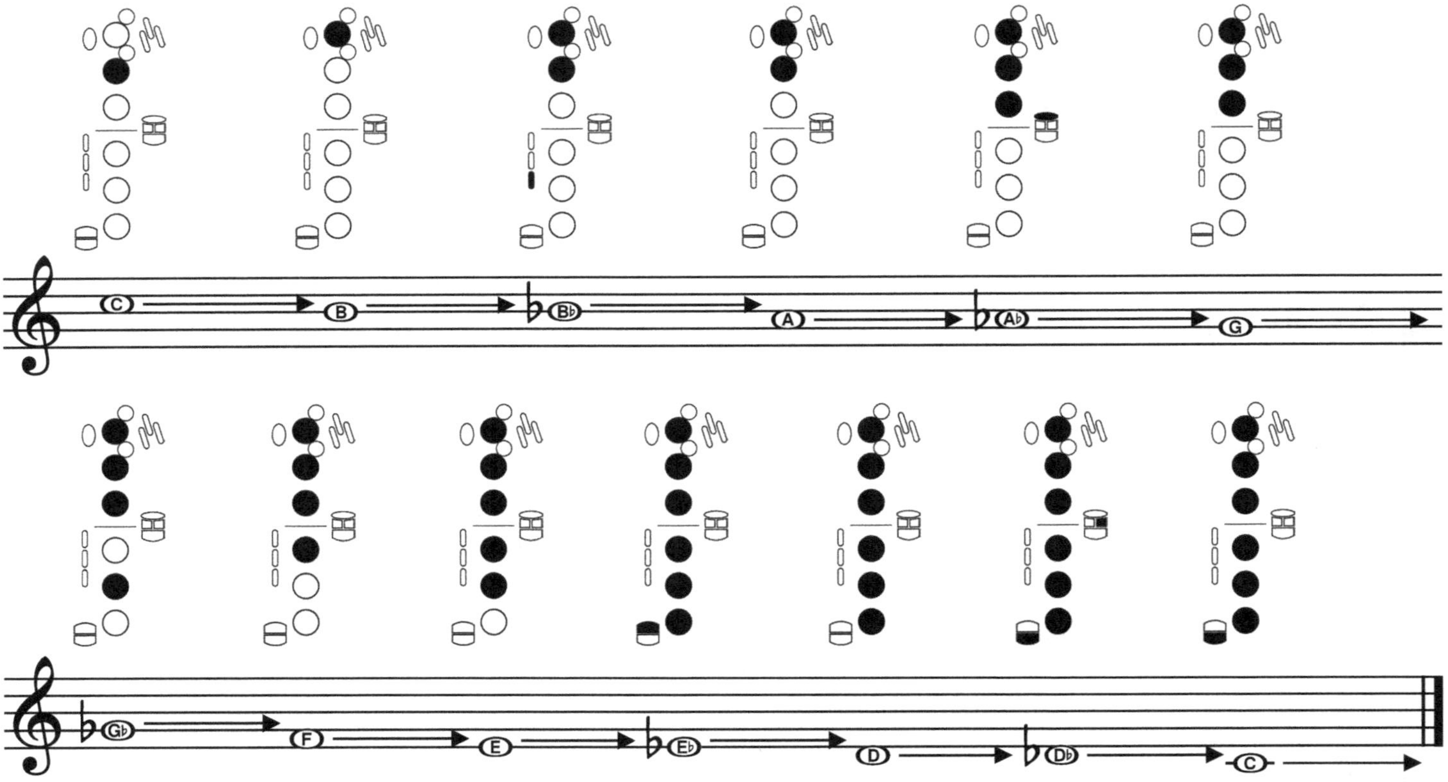

C B B♭ A A♭ G

G♭ F E E♭ D D♭ C

TUESDAY: CLASSICAL PIECE 359

Here is a piece in a classical style in the key of C major. If you need to look back in the book to remind yourself of ornamentation or trill fingerings, please do so.

WEDNESDAY: ARTICULATION 360

This piece is written in the key of D natural minor. Please pay special attention to the articulation.

THURSDAY: HARMONIC MINOR PIECE 361

Here is a nice piece in the key of F♯ harmonic minor for you to play today.

FRIDAY: SLOW BLUES PIECE 362

This is a slow blues piece. Listen to the recording to get yourself back into the mindset of swing articulation and feel.

SATURDAY: ii–V–I LICK 363

This is a ii–V–I progression in the key of F major. I've written in the articulation to help you, especially with the triplet section.

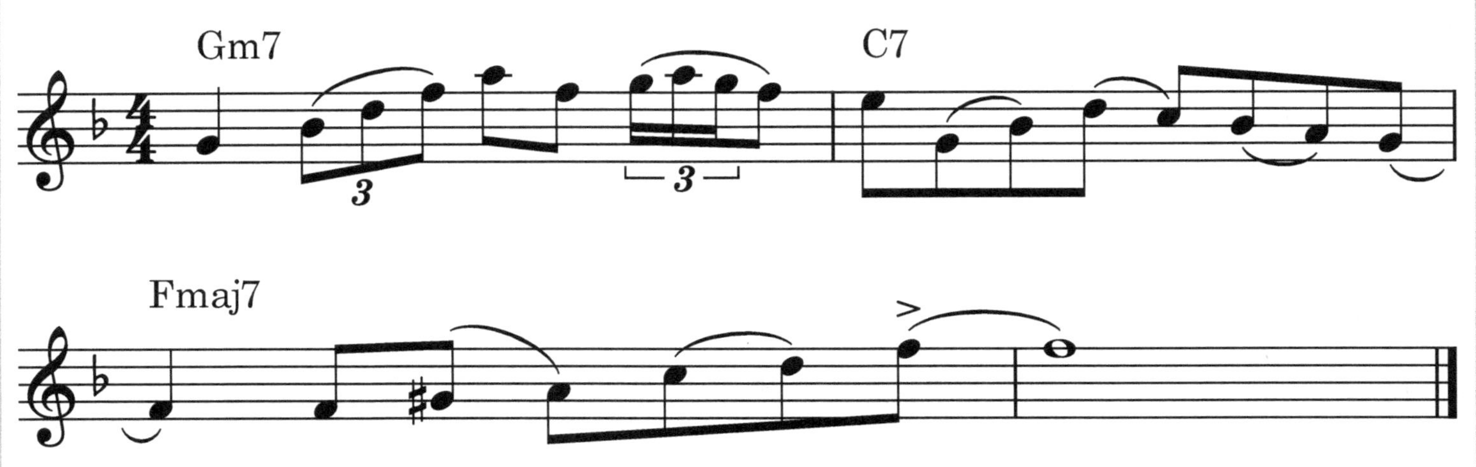

SUNDAY: iii–VI–ii–V–I LICK 364

Here is a iii–VI–ii–V–I piece in the key of C major. This should be played with a swing feel and swing articulation. Before you try it, listen to the recording to get an idea of the feel, tempo, and articulation.

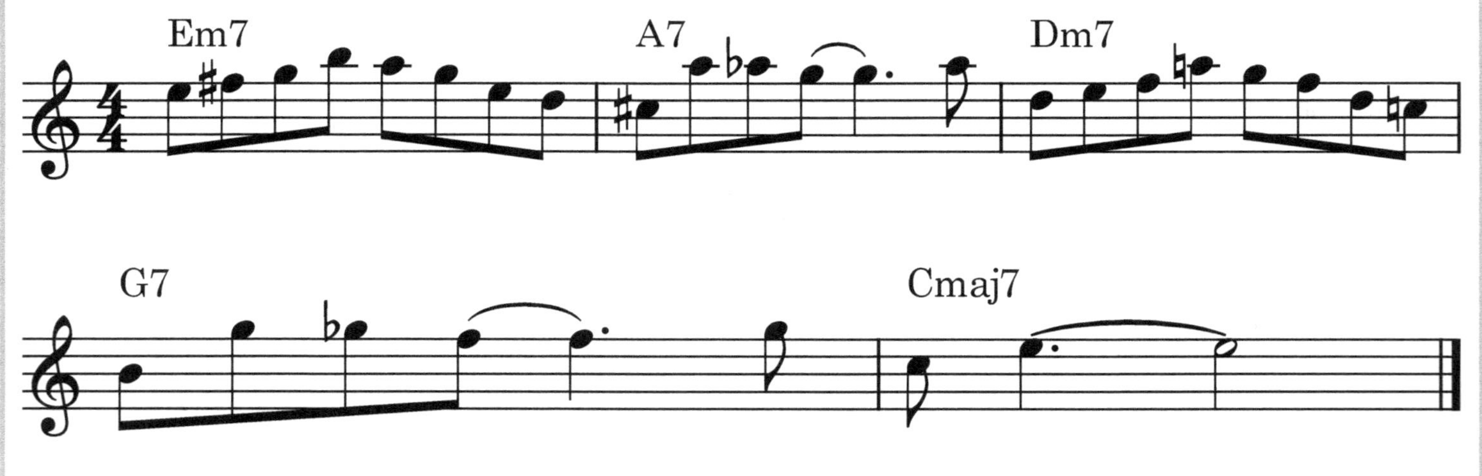

WEEK 53: DAY 365

MONDAY: ii–V LICKS 365

Wow! This is the last day! What a journey! I'm so happy that you made it to the end. For the last day, you'll play a ii–V lick that goes through six keys. Enjoy!

ABOUT THE AUTHOR

Aaron Gardner is the author of two bestsellers, *How to Play Alto Sax in 14 Days* and *How to Play Tenor Sax in 14 Days.* Aaron began taking private flute lessons in the fourth grade and hasn't stopped playing music since. After gaining a strong foundation in classical music, Aaron attended Berklee College of Music in Boston, where he studied jazz flute and saxophone with Joe Viola and George Garzone.

Today, he lives and works in Milwaukee, Wisconsin, where he teaches at the Wisconsin Conservatory of Music. He also uses his talents to fulfill a community need by sharing the joys of art and music with students in Milwaukee Public Schools. Aaron has recorded music for shows on Netflix and PBS, and performs in a variety of styles with many local and national acts, including the Violent Femmes and Willy Porter. He also teaches online lessons and can be reached via email at: *aarongardnerlessons@gmail.com*

www.ingramcontent.com/pod-product-compliance
Lightning Source LLC
LaVergne TN
LVHW081407110826
845149LV00010B/1663